Walking with the Word

Walking with the Word

Daily Ventures into 15 Books of the Bible

Br. Larry Schatz, FSC

Saint Mary's Press®

Dedication

To my sisters, Jane and Claudine,
and to all my Brothers

The publishing team included Laurie Delgatto, development editor; Lorraine Kilmartin, reviewer; cover image: iStockphoto/AVTG; prepress and manufacturing coordinated by the production departments of Saint Mary's Press.

Printed in the United States of America

3458

ISBN 978-0-88489-993-8

Library of Congress Cataloging-in-Publication Data

Schatz, Larry.
    Walking with the word : daily ventures into 15 books of the Bible / Larry Schatz.
       p. cm.
ISBN 978-0-88489-993-8 (pbk.)
    1. Bible—Devotional use. 2. Bible—Meditations. 3. Devotional calendars. 4. Teenagers—Religious life. I. Title.

BS617.8.S37 2008
242'.2—dc22

                                                 2007040211

Introduction

Whatever we call it—the Bible, the Scriptures, the Good Book—it remains a fascinating treasury of stories and wisdom. You are about to read, chapter by chapter, through fifteen books of the Bible. Though the books may seem randomly chosen, they actually represent a sample of all the major types of writing in the Bible. They are not arranged in chronological order, simply because they do not tell the story of salvation history from beginning to end. Luke is first, because for those of us who are followers of Christ, the Gospels are the definitive portrait of Jesus and how we can best get a sense of who Jesus is. You will encounter a mix of Old and New Testament books: history, prophets, wisdom literature, letters, and even some apocalyptic writing. The Bible is an endlessly fascinating account of humankind's encounter with the God revealed through Jesus. You will inevitably be more attracted to some books than others.

Begin your daily mediation by slowly reading the indicated Scripture passage. Then read through the reflection on that passage in this book. Finally, spend a few moments thinking about the passage. Be assured that a rich and rewarding journey awaits you. Have a wonderful walk with the Word!

Today's Scripture Passage
Luke 1:1–25

We all know how important the first sentence of a book is. Those well-chosen words could make us want to either read on or move on to another book. Imagine, then, how carefully the author of Luke's Gospel must have chosen his words, knowing the importance of his subject. The opening phrase lets us know that the Book of Luke is one of several accounts of the Good News. As Luke explains to Theophilus ("lover of God"), he intends to write an orderly version of the events that have been handed down. He clearly wants his readers to fully understand the real meaning of all the things they have heard about Jesus the Christ. And so, Luke starts from the beginning with the miraculous births of John the Baptist and his cousin Jesus of Nazareth and, true to his word, he uses an orderly structure to do it.

Think About . . .

Compare the opening sentence of Luke to the opening sentences of the other Gospels. What impressions do you have of each author?

Today's Scripture Passage
Luke 1:26–80

The heart and soul of this part of chapter 1 is verses 46–55, referred to as the *Magnificat*. Perhaps the similar word *magnificent* best describes this eloquent prayer of praise that Christians around the world recite every day in the Liturgy of the Hours. This prayer captures a major theme of Luke's Gospel: those who possess much in the world's eyes will find themselves with very little; the Savior will turn everything upside down. Mary realizes her own humility by expressing her lowliness, and yet she knows she will be called blessed. She proclaims that through Jesus's growing in her womb, God is fulfilling an ancient promise, and that this fulfillment will quite literally change the world. And indeed it does!

Think About . . .

What would you say to praise God's actions in your own life? Write down your words of praise.

Today's Scripture Passage
Luke 2:1–21

Whenever we see a crèche at Christmastime, it doesn't seem complete without a shepherd or two. It is important to understand that at the time of Jesus, shepherds were outcasts that were generally despised. They were definitely not part of the Jewish mainstream. Luke continually focuses on the Good News being given to those who are poor and downtrodden. Think about it: the first ones to hear the news of the birth of the long-awaited Messiah are the lowly shepherds out in their fields. The angel points them to the manger so they can be the first to witness the birth of the Lord. And it is entirely fitting that they should encounter a poor couple forced to lay their newborn in a manger, a feeding trough for cattle. This is just the opposite of what would be expected for the birth of the Savior.

Think About . . .

If Jesus were born today, to whom would the news of his birth be given and where would he be born?

Today's Scripture Passage
Luke 2:22–52

Here Luke provides us with the only Gospel story of Jesus as an adolescent. And, as so often is the case between adolescents and their parents, it involves worrying and misunderstanding. By deliberately staying behind in Jerusalem, Jesus put his parents through several days of fear and anxiety. When they finally find him, his response to their understandable concern is a very challenging one. Mary speaks of Jesus's earthly father, Joseph, but Jesus replies by referring to his heavenly Father. As all adolescents do, Jesus is beginning to explore the meaning of his own identity, one that will continually be misunderstood by people who are expecting a very different kind of Messiah. Jesus does, however, return home with his parents, obedient to them for many more years before beginning his public ministry.

Think About . . .

Spend some time reflecting on your own struggles with your parents or guardians as you grow into your identity. Ask Jesus to help you with your "growing pains."

Today's Scripture Passage

Luke, Chapter 3

Eighteen years have passed, and now Jesus is about to begin his public ministry. This chapter gives us a vivid portrait of Jesus's cousin, John the Baptist. John is preaching the need for repentance, and in verses 10–14, three times he is asked, "What should we do?" What is really being asked, of course, is, "What should we do to be saved?" And in each case, John gives very practical advice. Simply put, he tells his listeners to do the right thing and, especially for the tax collectors and soldiers, not to abuse their positions to become richer. As he does many times in his Gospel, Luke raises the point that wealth and possessions can easily keep us from growing in our faith. John is also clear that he is the forerunner to the Messiah, that he is only preparing the way by urging people to repent and be forgiven.

Think About . . .

What advice might John the Baptist give you if you asked him, "What should I do?"

Today's Scripture Passage
Luke 4:1–13

After forty days of fasting in the wilderness, who wouldn't be hungry? And really, what would be the harm in turning a stone into a loaf of bread? It would be kind of a cool trick, wouldn't it? Actually that's the problem here. If Jesus were to give in to this temptation, along with the other two he faces, he would be a totally different Messiah. He is essentially being asked to show off, to perform tricks that would be very impressive and would, no doubt, win people over. But Jesus is ready to begin his public ministry as a human being, as someone who has to deal with life and its temptations and distractions just as we do. By choosing to be one of us, he is also rejecting special treatment, or the easy way out. Jesus wants to show us the way of a servant who seeks to do good for others, not for himself.

Think About . . .

Why does it seem so much more appealing to be a celebrity rather than a servant?

Today's Scripture Passage
Luke 4:14–43

Where better for Jesus to begin his mission than in his hometown of Nazareth? After all, he grew up there, and everyone knows he is Joseph's son. So how does Jesus go from being the hometown hero to almost being thrown off a cliff within a couple verses? The answer probably has more to do with his listeners than with him. Clearly Jesus really impressed them in the synagogue with his message of the Good News. When he tries to get his old friends and neighbors to think bigger than just Nazareth, however, sparks begin to fly. It seems rather abrupt, but perhaps Luke is fore-shadowing what will happen to Jesus in Jerusalem: initial acceptance and enthusiasm followed by rejection and rage.

Think About . . .

Why is it that the people who know you best can sometimes be your harshest critics when you take a different path than they think you should?

Today's Scripture Passage
Luke, Chapter 5

It is hard for us to really imagine what it was like to have leprosy in the time of Jesus. Lepers were feared and were outcasts, banished to the fringes of society. No one wanted to be around them; they were considered unclean. It was best to just look the other way and not even get near someone with leprosy. Notice how much Luke tells us about Jesus in only a few short verses (see verses 12–16). The leper approaches Jesus, which was a bold move, and requests to be healed. Clearly he has heard that Jesus can work wonders. Not only does Jesus immediately respond to the man's request, but he actually touches the leper—an equally bold move and a powerful sign of how Jesus intends to break through barriers and stereotypes to let people know they are worthy of dignity and attention.

Think About . . .

In your neighborhood or school, to whom would Jesus reach out? Could you do the same?

Today's Scripture Passage
Luke, Chapter 6

The last part of this chapter (verses 43–49) deals with quality. Typical of Jesus, he uses everyday images—fruit trees and house foundations—to make his point. Have you ever noticed how most people pick out fruit in a grocery store? They generally pick up and put back a few before they find what they are looking for. They want the best looking fruit because they assume it will taste the best. And before people purchase a home, they generally check the basement or lower level to make sure it has a good foundation. If it doesn't, they look somewhere else, unless they are careless or in a hurry. The point is clear: quality matters. The foundation of a structure is the key to its strength and ability to last. Good trees bear good fruit. Solid foundations resist the forces of nature.

Think About . . .

What kind of foundation are you built on?
What happens when times get rough?

Today's Scripture Passage
Luke, Chapter 7

Hospitality. That really is the crux of the last section of this chapter. Jesus is invited into the home of a Pharisee named Simon. Then this woman shows up, and in an almost embarrassing display of affection, she bathes and kisses Jesus's feet. She is of course a woman "with a reputation." Simon can't believe Jesus doesn't know this. Ah, but that's precisely the point: Jesus *does* know this, and he uses this woman's repentance to drive home an important point in Luke's Gospel: even though Simon invites Jesus into his home, it is this sinful woman who makes Jesus feel welcome. Her emotional response to Jesus sharply contrasts with Simon's response. By welcoming this woman, Jesus reflects God's generosity and God's lavish love for us, especially when we seek forgiveness.

Think About . . .

Why is judging others a barrier to hospitality?

Today's Scripture Passage
Luke, Chapter 8

How can Jesus sleep that soundly? The boat is filling with water and obviously rocking heavily, and yet he is still fast asleep. What is this scene all about? For people in biblical times, water, especially a stormy sea with big waves, was a symbol of chaos. A boat often symbolized the early Church. Add to that the image of Jesus's commanding the wind to cease, which casts Jesus in the role of the Creator. The message is clear: No matter how dangerous or threatening things may seem to be in our faith journey, Jesus is always with us and will not let us go down. Even when it appears that Jesus is asleep or dormant, we can't forget that he is a powerful force in our lives and can calm any turbulence we may feel.

Think About . . .

Consider a tough time you've had recently. Now try to picture yourself with Jesus during that time. What might he say to you?

Today's Scripture Passage
Luke, Chapter 9

In verses 46–48, Jesus teaches his followers a vital lesson. At this point in the Gospel journey, they have been with him long enough to have seen him do some pretty amazing things. Three of them have just witnessed Jesus's Transfiguration. He has spoken about his suffering and death. And yet his followers really don't get it. We often see pictures of Jesus with children, and it's not hard to imagine that he loved to be in their presence, and they in his. And so he places a child next to himself to drive home the point about who is first, who is last, and who is the greatest of them all. Jesus came to upend all our assumptions about what is important. It is not one of the Apostles that Jesus puts by his side, but rather a little child. End of discussion. Status means nothing. Sincerity and trust, the qualities of childhood, mean everything.

Think About . . .

Reflect on the difference between being childlike and being childish.

Today's Scripture Passage
Luke, Chapter 10

The familiar parable of the good Samaritan appears only in Luke's Gospel. The problem is that the word *Samaritan* doesn't mean much to us. To the followers of Jesus, however, it is definitely not a neutral word. What Jesus is doing here is trying to vastly expand the concept of neighbor. The first two who pass by the nearly dead man do so out of a sense of following the Law and not wanting to be made unclean by having contact with someone who might be dead. So who stops to help? Who proves to be the true neighbor? It is the person we instinctively cast as an enemy, as a bad person. And suddenly the idea of loving your neighbor gets more challenging and unpleasant. The question becomes not what is the correct thing to do, but what is the right thing to do.

Think About . . .

Whom in my life, or in the world, do I have the hardest time seeing as my neighbor? Why?

Today's Scripture Passage
Luke, Chapter 11

This chapter begins with Luke's version of the most familiar prayer uniting all Christians: the Lord's Prayer. If you compare Luke's version with Matthew's (see 6:9–13), you'll notice that Luke's is more concise, although the same basic elements are in both. Luke focuses his attention solely on how to pray. He makes two points in his story about the friend who wants to borrow bread. The first point is that persistence is valuable. We don't hesitate to pester our parents or friends if we really want something. We shouldn't hesitate to "pester" God either. The second point is that as parents we would never deliberately give something harmful to our children. We are far from perfect, but we do know how to give our best to those we hold dear. Imagine, then, how much more eager and willing God is to do the same for us.

Think About . . .

Make a point of asking God every day to send you the Holy Spirit. How can you best remind yourself to do this?

Today's Scripture Passage
Luke, Chapter 12

Why is it that in our world the rich get richer?
Why are so many of us obsessed with the rich
and famous? What is it that causes the wealthy
to want to accumulate more and more? It's a big
problem in our society. We don't have to look far
for examples of corporate greed, of top execu-
tives acquiring much more than they'll ever need.
The story of the rich fool drives home the point of
how foolish it is to let greed take us over. Our first
priority should be God. If we are greedy for anything, we should be greedy to acquire a deeper
relationship with God, for the ability to trust in
God above all else. Easier said than done, of
course, especially in a world so obsessed with
security and inheritance. Jesus tells us our hearts
will follow our riches. Where is our true wealth?

Think About . . .

Make a list of your priorities in life. How many
of them involve money?

Today's Scripture Passage
Luke, Chapter 13

Mustard seed and yeast. It's pretty clear what they have in common. Both are small and seemingly insignificant. Both also hold tremendous potential for growth. Of course, they have to be given a chance by either being planted or activated. Without an agent—someone to plant the seed or mix the yeast into the dough—nothing will happen. So what do these two parables tell us about the Kingdom of God? Perhaps that each of us has a vital role to play in bringing about the Reign of God. Also perhaps that the Reign of God grows in a quiet, barely noticeable way. It's the little things that count. It's the small gestures that can make a huge difference. Slowly, steadily, the little things add up. The seed becomes a tree. The yeast transforms dough into bread. The world changes for the better because we have done something good.

Think About . . .

Reflect on some small acts of kindness that have made a difference in your life or in the life of someone you know.

Today's Scripture Passage
Luke, Chapter 14

There certainly is a focus on eating and feasts in this chapter. What is going on here? For one thing, it is necessary to understand how important hospitality is in Jesus's time. The sharing of meals occurs over and over throughout the Bible because eating is such a basic and vital part of being human and meals are meant to be shared. So who gets invited and how they respond and where they are seated all come into play here as Jesus weaves a couple parables into his teachings. One speaks of humility and how Jesus reverses what seems proper. Typical of Luke's Gospel, it is those who are poor and marginalized—"the least"—who end up coming to the banquet and being seated in the best seats. Jesus challenges us to seek out and invite those very people into our lives rather than all the people who can and will repay us with an invitation in turn.

Think About . . .

How well do you make others feel "at home"? Whom do you know that is an expert at hospitality?

Today's Scripture Passage
Luke, Chapter 15

This chapter of the Book of Luke features three parables with the same theme of lost and found: a sheep, a coin, and a son. The third parable, unique to the Book of Luke, is a familiar and rich one, but it really is much more complex than it first seems, mainly because of the older son and his resentment. Note how in each parable, there is great joy and celebration when what was lost is found. In fact, it actually seems a bit extravagant, doesn't it? A woman throws a party because she finds a lost coin. The father actually runs out to greet his son and doesn't even let him finish his apology. He throws a huge party. It's the extravagance here that Jesus is emphasizing. Could it be true that God is really that accepting and loves us that much, especially when we have strayed and returned again? Yes, it's true!

Think About . . .

Try to picture God with arms wide open to embrace you and welcome you back. Try also to understand the older son's resentment at the extravagant love of his father.

Today's Scripture Passage
Luke, Chapter 16

The parable of the rich man and Lazarus is about the have's and the have-nots, and the great gap that exists between the two. Typical to Luke, the order is reversed upon death. Now Lazarus has it all, and the rich man has nothing. It's not that the rich man is a bad man; rather, it's simply that he never even notices Lazarus. He is so insulated from anything but his own luxury that he can't see beyond all he has. Therein lies his downfall. He simply doesn't notice a poor man at his gate. He never crosses over the great divide. When he dies, he so wants to warn his brothers to notice those who are poor among them, but they have the same opportunities he had. How can we truly follow Christ if we are so caught up in the things of this world that we don't even notice those who go without?

Think About . . .

Being a Christian means being attentive. Try to make that your mantra today. Notice. Pay attention.

Today's Scripture Passage
Luke, Chapter 17

The parable of the grateful Samaritan appears only in the Book of Luke. Notice that once again, it is a Samaritan who stands apart as the righteous one. Back in chapter 10, we read the parable of the good Samaritan. Now we read about ten lepers who are cured by Jesus. Only one returns to thank Jesus, and this one is a detested Samaritan. Talk about being an outsider. First, he has leprosy, which means he is automatically shunned and avoided. Then he is a Samaritan, which means he is automatically shunned and avoided by all Jews. Yet it is this man, the ultimate outsider, who comes back to fall at Jesus's feet, who is full of gratitude. Why is Luke so intent on portraying Jesus as the one who reaches out to the most marginalized? In many ways, the early Christians Luke was writing for were also outsiders.

Think About . . .

Make a point of being grateful today, and expressing your gratitude, especially to those people who often go unnoticed by others.

Today's Scripture Passage
Luke, Chapter 18

By now you have probably figured out that Luke loves to show how earthly standards and expectations are reversed by God. The parable of the Pharisee and the tax collector is another prime example of Luke at his best. Clearly the Pharisee is doing everything right and following the Law. And just as clearly, the tax collector, by his profession, is collaborating with the Romans, the enemy. Imagine how shocked the Pharisee would be to learn that God favored the tax collector! The theme of humility appears again as well. Really, who can brag about being good before God, who knows us better than we know ourselves? People who are convinced of their own righteousness end up losing out to those who admit before God that they have a long way to go.

Think About . . .

Why is it that some people who call themselves good Christians often become so judgmental of others? What is the attitude of a true follower of Jesus?

Today's Scripture Passage
Luke, Chapter 19

Jesus is getting very close to Jerusalem and his final days. He is passing through Jericho, the last town before his triumphal entry into his city of destiny. It is there that he encounters an interesting little man named Zacchaeus, who is determined to catch a glimpse of the now famous Jesus. However, it seems a bit much for someone of Zacchaeus's profession and wealth to climb a tree. That's the point. Even though Zacchaeus is small in stature, he clearly has a big heart. Jesus senses this and once again confounds everyone around him by inviting himself to Zacchaeus's home. Zacchaeus is happy with and touched by Jesus's attention to him. It's almost as if Jesus has radar for the big sinners who have big hearts. Though everyone grumbles, Jesus has just expanded the Reign of God a little further.

Think About . . .

What role has determination played in your life so far?

Today's Scripture Passage
Luke, Chapter 20

Jesus is now in Jerusalem for Passover. In verses 1–8 and again in verses 19–26, Jesus is confronted by the Jewish authorities, who try to undermine him. They ask him loaded questions, hoping to trap him. It doesn't work, of course. Both times Jesus gets the better of them, either by asking them a question in return or by refusing to be forced into a simple answer, as in the case of paying Roman taxes. Keep in mind that these confrontations occur in public places in a crowded city, so many people hear the exchange. It is not hard to see why the authorities are getting so frustrated with Jesus. His cleverness and refusal to be backed into a corner are impressing people. He's clearly the man of the hour.

Think About . . .

How have you dealt with confrontation?
Would you handle it differently next time?

Today's Scripture Passage
Luke, Chapter 21

This is a challenging chapter, as Jesus speaks of destruction and suffering and the Son of Man. It's important to realize that Luke wrote his Gospel sometime after AD 80, which is after Jerusalem and the Temple were destroyed. In verses 7–19, Jesus speaks words of encouragement for his followers. Rough times are ahead. Lots of people will hate you. You'll be arrested and imprisoned. But don't worry about a thing. It's going to be okay. Hang in there. All of us need to hear those words at times, but imagine how much they mean to the early Christians, who are surrounded by hostile forces.

Think About . . .

What advice do you think Jesus would give to his followers today?

Today's Scripture Passage
Luke, Chapter 22

Let us focus our attention on Luke's version of what is commonly called the agony in the garden. For Luke, the theme of prayer is very prominent here. The word *prayer* is mentioned several times in the seven verses that describe the scene. Clearly this episode, more than any other in the Passion stories, shows Jesus's humanity. He prays hard that he can accept his Father's will. We see the intensity of prayer with Jesus's sweat becoming like drops of blood on the ground. Sweat is a sign of deep anxiety, and to sweat this much proves that Jesus is indeed struggling with what lies ahead. He prays to prevail, and he does. But notice that it is in prayer that he accomplishes the strength to go on. At the beginning and end of the scene, he tells his disciples to pray so that they can avoid temptation.

Think About . . .

We usually turn to prayer during times of great stress. Why is that? Is that true for you?

Today's Scripture Passage
Luke, Chapter 23

Let us focus on Luke's account of the Crucifixion and death of Jesus. Notice the words of Jesus in verses 27–46. They are all words of compassion and forgiveness and prayer. There are no words of despair or sorrow. Luke is showing us a Jesus and a Messiah who is in control until the end. He survived the temptation to back away from his fate, and now he surrenders to his Father's will. Luke downplays Jesus's suffering so that even at the moment of his death, Jesus is able to cry out to his Father in a loud voice before taking his last breath. As soon as Jesus dies, a Roman centurion is the first to acknowledge his innocence. This is important because the Christians that Luke was writing for were mainly Gentiles, or non-Jews, so he is conscious of Jesus's being recognized as the Messiah by all people.

Think About . . .

Spend some time reflecting on Jesus's last words in verse 46. Why is this a powerful prayer for all Christians?

Today's Scripture Passage
Luke, Chapter 24

Luke is at his best here. The heart of the story is that these two disillusioned followers of Jesus recognize him, finally, in the breaking of the bread. At that moment, their eyes are opened and their hearts are burning, knowing they have had an encounter with the risen Lord. So why does Jesus vanish at that moment of recognition? What is the message to Luke's readers, and to us? Most of us are so used to the Eucharist that we don't give a lot of thought to what it really is and what it means. Even though Jesus is not physically present in our lives, he is nonetheless very much with us, as he was with the early Christians. Often the Eucharist is described by Catholics as the "Real Presence." This is a powerful way of saying the truth of this story. In the sharing of the Eucharist, Jesus is with us.

Think About . . .

Consider a time when your eyes were opened, when you realized a truth you had not grasped before. What opened your eyes?

Today's Scripture Passage
1 Samuel, Chapter 1

With the books of Samuel, we start a study of the beginning of the monarchy in Israel. David, who reigned from about 1080 BC to 1040 BC, is at the heart of these books. But first we learn about the prophet for whom these books are named. The first chapter of 1 Samuel tells us about Hannah, one of the wives of Elkanah. She is unable to bear children. Throughout the Bible, infertility is considered a curse. Hannah prays hard, and finally her prayers are answered. She gives birth to Samuel, and she dedicates him to the Lord. Because of that, she leaves her very young son with the priest Eli at Shiloh, which was the most important shrine in Israel at the time. This may seem strange to us, but it is Hannah's way of thanking God for the long-awaited gift of her son. She knows he will always be in good hands because he is in a holy place. Hannah never gives up, and her persistence in prayer pays off.

Think About . . .

What are you praying for these days? How persistent are you?

Today's Scripture Passage
1 Samuel, Chapter 2

Hannah's prayer is significant for several reasons. You may have noticed how similar it is to Mary's prayer (the *Magnificat*) in Luke 1:46–55. Both begin with praise for the Lord and then go into a series of parallel verses that contrast the have's with the have-nots, and how God will reverse their situations. They emphasize the raising up of those who are poor. Hannah speaks from her heart because she was unable to have children and now has borne a son. As we find out later in the chapter, she is graced with five more children because of her faithfulness to God. The rest of the chapter deals with the contrast between the goodness of young Samuel and the evil actions of Eli's two sons.

Think About . . .

Reread Mary's prayer and note the lines and phrases that are almost identical to Hannah's prayer. Notice the confidence and joy both express.

Today's Scripture Passage

1 Samuel, Chapter 3

The story of Samuel's call is a beautiful one, plac-ing Samuel in the great tradition of other prophets who received calls, such as Isaiah, Jeremiah, and Ezekiel. The fact that Samuel gets his call while sleeping places him in another biblical tradition: that God at times speaks to people in their dreams. The fact that Samuel does not at first recognize the voice of God, that Eli is the one who counsels him to respond by addressing the Lord directly, shows that Eli, as Samuel's mentor, realizes that this marks the end of his own impor-tance and the beginning of Samuel's vocation as a prophet. Indeed once Samuel responds directly to God's call, he is given a prophetic message. This is also a reminder that we often need others to help us discern God's call in our own lives.

Think About . . .

Make Samuel's simple response to God's call (see verse 10) your own prayer today. Or maybe even for the rest of your life!

Today's Scripture Passage

1 Samuel, Chapter 4

In this chapter, we read about the death of Eli, his two sons, and his daughter-in-law, plus many Israelites in battle. But the real tragedy, and the one that leads to Eli's death, is the news that the ark of the Covenant has been captured by the Philistines. It is hard for us to imagine what a tragic event this is for Israel. The ark is the holiest object in the Jewish faith; it represents God's abiding presence with the people. That is why they always bring it with them into battle, to ensure that God will be with them. This is the ark fashioned during the time of Moses to hold the Ten Commandments. The fact that the enemies of the Israelites have stolen the ark is almost too much to bear, certainly for Eli. The last words of Eli's daughter-in-law at the end of the chapter sum up how everyone feels.

Think About . . .

What in your life represents God's holy presence for you?

Today's Scripture Passage
1 Samuel, Chapter 5

It doesn't take long for the Philistines to realize that maybe taking the ark from the Israelites wasn't such a great idea after all. The first part of the chapter is basically a contest between deities. The Philistines place the ark near Dagon as a sort of offering, but they discover the next day that the idol Dagon has fallen before the ark. The following day, the same thing happens, but this time the head and hands are broken off too. The implication is clear: Dagon is no match for the God of the Israelites. They decide to move the ark, but wherever it ends up, the people are stricken with tumors (some Bible translations say they were hemorrhoids). The writers of the First Book of Samuel are clearly showing that the Philistines are suffering the effects of their actions. They steal the ark, expecting it will solidify their victory over Israel. Instead it brings them nothing but trouble.

Think About . . .

When have you been forced to deal with the consequences of your actions?

Today's Scripture Passage

1 Samuel, Chapter 6

After seven months with the ark, the Philistines have had enough. They consult with experts on how best to return this holy object they stole from Israel. They end up giving gifts of gold in the shape of tumors and mice. This has led some Scripture scholars to connect the suffering of the Philistines with a plague carried by mice. The Philistines also send the ark in a cart pulled by cows, without any human intervention, to determine whether the God of Israel is indeed responsible for what happened to them. The cows go toward Beth-shemesh—that is, toward the Israelites. The Philistines get their answer. When the Israelites see the ark, they rejoice and sacrifice the cows as a burnt offering to God, a common practice in biblical times.

Think About . . .

The people of Old Testament times believed very much in the necessity of sacrifice as part of worshiping God. We no longer sacrifice animals. What are other ways of sacrificing?

Today's Scripture Passage
1 Samuel, Chapter 7

Samuel is the last of the judges of Israel; however, the term *judge* as it is used here is very different from modern-day usage of the word. A judge at this time in biblical history is actually a type of tribal leader and often a military hero as well. At this point in their history, the Israelites have no unified nation. There is no one ruler. Judges arise whenever Israel is attacked, and they lead the people in battle. We have already been intro-duced to Samuel as a prophet. He also takes on the role of judge to lead the people against their persistent enemies, the Philistines. The last verse indicates that Samuel administers justice in his home at Ramah, so he also serves in the role of judge that we are familiar with. Samuel serves as a bridge between the time of the judges and the time of the kings.

Think About . . .

Who are the leaders you know (or have read about) that demonstrate a variety of skills?

Today's Scripture Passage
1 Samuel, Chapter 8

At the heart of this chapter is a basic conflict, which isn't quite resolved. The people want a king, but Samuel tries to convince them that is a bad idea. By desiring a king, they are in effect rejecting God as their king, and that is a problem for Samuel. All the other nations have kings to lead them, so why shouldn't Israel? Samuel tries to warn them that by having a king, they will have to give up a lot, especially the independence and freedom they are used to. But Samuel's detailed list of what will result fails to dissuade the people. So they get their way; God tells Samuel to appoint a king over them. It is clear that neither Samuel nor God is pleased with this development.

Think About . . .

Recall a time when you got something you really wanted, only to discover later that it wasn't all that great. Why does that happen?

Today's Scripture Passage
1 Samuel, Chapter 9

In this chapter, we are introduced to the man who will become the first king of Israel. He introduces himself as Saul from the Tribe of Benjamin. Because Benjamin is the youngest of Jacob's sons, the tribe is considered "the least" of the tribes. This indicates, as happens so often in Scripture, that Saul is not an obvious choice to be king. Yet early in the chapter, we are told that Saul is handsome and tall, both typical "kingly" characteristics. His journey to find the lost donkeys has an epic flavor to it. It could almost be a whole novel in itself, as Saul encounters Samuel, who has been told by God that this young man is the one God has chosen to be king. Saul is then treated like a king with a special feast given in his honor.

Think About . . .

A journey undertaken to seek something and then ending up with something very different is a common theme in literature and stories. Reflect on why this is so.

Today's Scripture Passage
1 Samuel, Chapter 10

Things get a little confusing in this chapter. It is almost as if the story of Saul starts over in verse 17. What is going on here? Most likely, there are two versions about how Saul becomes king. The author is probably familiar with both, and tries to reconcile them here. The first part continues the hero story that begins in chapter 9 with the Spirit's rushing upon Saul, a sure sign of God's favor. The second part resumes the theme from chapter 8 about the uneasiness Samuel feels about choosing a king. Nevertheless, Saul is clearly God's choice, and the ritual of anointing is the Jewish equivalent of crowning a king today. Being anointed means having oil poured on one's head. The chapter ends by setting the stage for Saul's first challenge: defeating the brutal Ammonites.

Think About . . .

How is oil used today in religious ritual? Why do you think oil is still used as a symbol of God's Spirit and anointing?

Today's Scripture Passage
1 Samuel, Chapter 11

Here Saul has the opportunity to prove himself as a warrior and hero, essential traits for an ancient king. He is actually taking on the role of the judges who preceded him as he attempts to unite all the tribes through battle. The action of cutting the oxen into pieces and sending them around Israel as a warning may strike us as strange, but this is a graphic way of getting across the message that everyone is needed and better show up to fight the Ammonites. And so they do. Saul is successful and is then made king. Wait . . . isn't he already the king? This episode seems to indicate that at this point, his kingship is made public and is accepted by the people. And now everyone seems happy. King Saul is the man of the hour!

Think About . . .

One of the essential traits of a leader is to unify his or her people. How do leaders accomplish that in our nation? in our world? in our Church?

Today's Scripture Passage
1 Samuel, Chapter 12

This is Samuel's farewell speech, although for the time being, he isn't going anywhere. He is "passing the torch" to Saul, the new king, and ending an era. The time of the judges in Israel is now over. The people have requested and received a king. Again Samuel points out that there really is no need for a king because God has taken care of them and has appointed leaders when needed. But because there is a king now, the people need to make sure they remain faithful to God and the Covenant. If they do that, things will go well. If they don't, the opposite will happen. It's that simple. Samuel will remain in their midst as a prophet and as someone who prays for them. In his prophetic role, he will serve as an intermediary between God and the people.

Think About . . .

Try to regularly pray for groups of people — in your neighborhood, your school, and your church, for example. What other groups can you pray for?

Today's Scripture Passage
1 Samuel, Chapter 13

Saul's main duty as king is to defend his people against their enemies. However, as Saul is preparing for battle with the Philistines, something happens that changes his destiny forever. The tradition is that only the prophets and priests can offer sacrifice before battle. Samuel has told Saul to wait seven days for his arrival, but when Samuel doesn't show up on time, and his troops are getting restless, Saul performs the sacrifice himself. When Samuel finds out what Saul has done, he tells him that because he has disobeyed, he has lost favor with God. Saul's dynasty would have lasted forever, which is typical of kingship—that it passes on in a family. Because of his actions, however, that will not happen. The point is that Saul disobeyed the Lord. He has therefore doomed his own reign.

Think About . . .

When have you disobeyed and had to deal with the consequences?

Today's Scripture Passage
1 Samuel, Chapter 14

It is clear that Saul's son Jonathan is a brave and
shrewd warrior, as demonstrated in the first part
of chapter 14. Later on, however, Jonathan eats
some honey, unaware that his father has forbidden the troops to eat before evening. When the
soldiers see this, they are fearful. What it finally
comes down to is that even though he did not
know he was doing wrong, Jonathan did go
against his father's orders, and when, through a
process similar to drawing lots, Jonathan is shown
to be guilty, he readily admits his guilt and his
willingness to die. The soldiers step in and ran-
som him, mainly because of his courage and success. What is the meaning of all this? Perhaps to
show that because he also disobeyed, Jonathan
is not fit to be king. This does support Samuel's
prophecy that Saul's sons would not succeed him.

Think About . . .

We often hear the phrase "Ignorance of the
law is no excuse." Does this make sense to
you? Why or why not?

Today's Scripture Passage
1 Samuel, Chapter 15

Saul really blows it this time. Samuel tells him to utterly wipe out the Amalekites for their opposition to the Israelites when they left Egypt. But Saul sets aside some of the best sheep and cattle for sacrifice to God, and he spares Agag, the Amalekite king. This is the final straw. Samuel tells Saul, in no uncertain terms, that because he has rejected God through his disobedience, God has rejected him. What Saul does may not seem so bad to us, but the fact that he has disobeyed is the issue. At this point in biblical history, obedience is of the utmost importance and is the truest way of being faithful. Because Saul has disobeyed a command, he is finished. When Saul accidentally rips Samuel's robe, Samuel tells him this symbolizes how God has torn the kingdom of Israel from him.

Think About . . .

Why is obedience so important?

Today's Scripture Passage
1 Samuel, Chapter 16

Because God rejects Saul, Samuel is sent to anoint the next king. The only problem is that Saul is still alive, and as long as he is alive, he remains king. Nevertheless young David is the one chosen to succeed him. Like Saul, David is not an obvious choice. He is the youngest of many brothers, and he is not even present when Samuel comes to Jesse's home to choose the next king. Remember that the oldest son always inherits the title and possessions of his father. Verse 7 reminds us that it's what is in the heart that counts, and only God knows that. David is seen as a man after God's own heart. There is irony in the fact that shortly after, David ends up being Saul's musician and then his armor bearer. At this point, Saul does not know David has already been anointed, but this gives David an opportunity to shine in several ways.

Think About . . .

Look into your own heart for a moment. What do you see there? What do you think God sees there?

Today's Scripture Passage
1 Samuel, Chapter 17

The story of David and Goliath is one of the best known in the Bible. The message is obvious: With God on our side, we can face huge challenges and overcome them. David displays here all the marks of greatness—unusual courage, military skill, and a deep, unwavering faith in God. The story seems to confirm him as the right choice to be the next king. If you read the text closely, you may notice that parts of this story seem to contradict what happened in the previous chapter. It's as if David just wandered onto the battle scene, with no previous connection to Saul. Most likely, there are two different oral traditions about David. Today editors are careful to make sure a story has consistency and flow. The ancient writers of the Bible did not think that way. They had no problem putting two stories side by side, with contrasting details. This happens fairly often in the Scriptures.

Think About . . .

What is a Goliath in your life right now? How can your faith in God help you overcome this challenge?

Today's Scripture Passage
1 Samuel, Chapter 18

David's star is shining brightly. His best friend and closest ally is Jonathan, Saul's son. He marries Michal, Saul's daughter. He is successful in battle; the people love him. Clearly David is the man of the hour. Saul is overtaken with jealousy and by the end of the chapter becomes David's sworn enemy. Surely Saul senses that, as promised by Samuel, God's favor has departed from Saul and is now with David. Seemingly, David can do no wrong, and Saul can only watch as David wins over his son, his daughter, and the love of the people. We can understand Saul's feeling threatened by David's fame and success. Who wouldn't be? But Saul lets his own insecurity overtake him. He becomes obsessed with destroying David and, in the process, will destroy himself.

Think About . . .

When have you found yourself in a position where nothing seemed to go right for you, while someone else got all the breaks? How did you handle that?

Today's Scripture Passage
1 Samuel, Chapter 19

Saul's obsession with David is played out in this chapter. First, Jonathan tries to convince his father that David has done nothing to harm him. In verse 6, Saul actually takes an oath not to put David to death. But after David's next victory over the Philistines, Saul hurls a spear at David while David is playing music. From then on, David stays out of Saul's sight. Determined to kill David, Saul sends messengers to David's house, but Michal uses deception to help her husband escape. David flees to Ramah and stays with Samuel. The rather strange ending to the chapter seems to indicate that even the Spirit of the Lord keeps Saul from David. Saul gets caught up in a prophetic frenzy and ends up naked, possibly a symbol that he has been stripped of his authority as king.

Think About . . .

Why is deception a bad choice?

Today's Scripture Passage
1 Samuel, Chapter 20

There is perhaps no stronger example and expression of deep friendship in the Bible than that between David and Jonathan. The love they share is clear when they say goodbye to each other at the end of the chapter. Adding to the significance of their friendship is the realization that, if not for David's anointing, Jonathan would become the next king of Israel. Jonathan has every reason in the world to resent David and to be as jealous as his father. Saul even points this out to Jonathan in verse 31. But Jonathan's loyalty to his friend outweighs any personal ambition he might have toward the kingship. He now knows that his father is determined to kill David, and he must take sides. He takes David's side against his own father. Jonathan and David have made a covenant of friendship that no one can break. True and lasting friendship is a rare thing.

Think About . . .

What can you do to deepen and strengthen the friendships you have?

Today's Scripture Passage

1 Samuel, Chapter 21

Two important developments occur here. Ahime-lech, the high priest of Nob, gives David and his men holy bread to eat. This is unusual, because at the time the sacred bread was given to priests only. David also receives the sword of Goliath. By his receiving both of these, it is as if David is also receiving the approval of the priests, the holy men of Israel. This is another important step for the future king. When David arrives in Gath, he pretends to be mad so he will not be harmed by the Philistines, especially when they see him with Goliath's sword. David makes up a story to get the holy bread, and here he pretends to be crazy; both are acts of deception, which seem questionable, except that the writer seems to imply that because David is fleeing Saul, he is justi-fied doing what he can to survive.

Think About . . .

At times a leader needs to be shrewd in order to survive. What examples can you think of when Jesus was shrewd?

Today's Scripture Passage
1 Samuel, Chapter 22

Recall how in chapter 15 Saul spares the king of the Amalekites. Now, however, he has no qualms about slaughtering all the priests of Nob, along with the entire city. In effect, he has wiped out the priesthood of Israel, all to take revenge on Ahimelech for helping David. Notice how the king's servants will not carry out Saul's orders. However, Doeg, the Edomite who was in Nob and told Saul about what happened, has no problem murdering hundreds of innocent people. One priest does escape, of course, and flees to David. This is important, because now the priesthood will survive with David's help, another blow to Saul's authority.

Think About . . .

What is it in humans that allows them to turn off their moral compasses and commit evil acts? Is "I was just following orders" a legitimate excuse?

Today's Scripture Passage

1 Samuel, Chapter 23

By the end of this chapter, Saul is clearly closing in on David and his troops. Only an unexpected attack by the Philistines diverts Saul and allows David to escape. Before this Jonathan once again swore his loyalty to David and told David he is very content to be his number two man. And so they renew their covenant of friendship with each other. Notice how many times in the chapter David turns directly to the Lord for help. Notice also that he receives guidance each time. This is important because it shows that David stays connected to God as he plans what to do next. By the way, the ephod in verse 6 refers to the garments a priest would wear. Abiathar, the only surviving priest, brings the ephod with him into David's presence.

Think About . . .

Do you turn to God before making decisions in your life? How have you experienced God's response?

Today's Scripture Passage

1 Samuel, Chapter 24

In this key encounter between David and Saul, David definitely has the upper hand. He has the perfect opportunity to finish off Saul, but instead he cuts off a corner of Saul's cloak without Saul's knowledge. As soon as David returns to the back of the cave, however, he is filled with remorse for doing even that. But the piece of Saul's cloak enables David to confront Saul and prove that even though he had the chance, he did not harm the Lord's anointed one. David even bows low to the ground to show his respect for Saul. When Saul realizes the truth of David's words, he cries and acknowledges that David has done the right thing. He states clearly that he knows David will be the next king, and he actually pleads with David not to kill his descendants, so that his name will not be entirely wiped out. This is a big step for Saul, as he faces up to the truth of his destiny.

Think About . . .

How do you balance respect for authority with your own disagreement or dissatisfaction with that authority?

Today's Scripture Passage
1 Samuel, Chapter 25

Nabal's name means "fool," and he does seem to live up to his name as he foolishly refuses David's request for hospitality. David swears vengeance, but Abigail, who is just the opposite of her husband, intervenes. She brings gifts to David and his men and begs him not to take revenge on her husband. David listens to her wise request and backs down. He admits that her good sense has prevented him from committing a bloody act of revenge without consulting the Lord. After Nabal's death, David takes Abigail to be his wife. He also marries Ahinoam, and we learn that he has given Michal to another man. This says a lot about how women were regarded in biblical times. David's marriages probably helped him gain political support in the territories of both women.

Think About . . .

Why is helping to make peace between two people an important role for followers of Jesus?

Today's Scripture Passage
1 Samuel, Chapter 26

Does this story sound familiar? Once again, as in chapter 24, we read an account of David's sparing Saul's life. As happens so often in the Bible, we probably have two different versions of a single event. The writers include both, and there are some key differences. Here David actually goes to where Saul is, rather than the chance encounter in chapter 24. Here Abishai offers to kill Saul, which would technically absolve David of his death. Again David resists but directs Abishai to take Saul's spear and water jug, much to the embarrassment of Abner, his bodyguard. So once again David declares his innocence and refuses to take Saul's life, even though he is given the chance. Again Saul relents and blesses David.

Think About . . .

Responding to evil with goodness is challenging, and yet it is what we are called to do. Think about some practical ways to do that in your own life.

Today's Scripture Passage
1 Samuel, Chapter 27

Deciphering the meaning of this chapter is a bit of a challenge; even Scripture scholars struggle with it. What happens is quite clear. David leaves Israel to get away from Saul and serves Achish, a Philistine king. In turn he is given Ziklag, which remained part of Israel after that. From there he raids three of Israel's enemies and leaves no one alive. What he tells Achish is that he destroyed Israelite settlements. Clearly David is deceiving his host. And no one is left alive to report what really happened. Why does David do this? Most likely, he is preparing for his own kingship by destroying the enemies of Israel, and by deceiving Achish, he is protecting himself in exile. This is certainly not David's finest hour.

Think About . . .

There are hundreds of thousands of people living in exile right now around the world. What exiles are you aware of? Take a moment to pray for all people who are living in exile.

Today's Scripture Passage
1 Samuel, Chapter 28

The main part of this chapter is about Saul's desperation. He is frightened by the upcoming battle with the Philistines. He has asked the Lord for help in all the traditional ways, but he has gotten no response. So he consults a medium. He has to leave Israel because mediums and wizards are forbidden there, as a violation of God's law. Saul goes to Endor and asks the medium to call forth Samuel. And so the ghost of Samuel appears, upset at being disturbed. Saul asks Samuel what he should do. The answer is no surprise. We know by now that Saul has been rejected and abandoned by God and so there is no hope for victory. In fact, the ghost of Samuel tells him he will die in battle the next day along with his sons. All that is left now is for the tragic events to play themselves out.

Think About . . .

Recall a time when you asked God for something and God did not grant your request. What did you receive instead?

Today's Scripture Passage
1 Samuel, Chapters 29–30

David is spared the dilemma of having to fight against his own people because the Philistine commanders refuse to go into battle with him and his troops. He returns to Ziklag only to find it has been plundered by the Amalekites, and all the women and children have been taken captive. Before deciding what to do, David consults with God. God tells him to pursue the Amalekites. Thanks to a servant of the Amalekites, David finds out where they are and swoops down on a celebration to recapture all that has been taken, including his two wives. His final act is to ensure that all who are part of his military force are treated fairly, whether they actually see combat or not. By the end of the chapter, David receives tribute from many parts of Israel. He is ready to become king.

Think About . . .

Based on all you have read, what kind of king do you think David will be?

Today's Scripture Passage

1 Samuel, Chapter 31

Saul comes to the end of his days. It is difficult not to feel some compassion for him, despite all he has done wrong. His three sons are killed, and Saul himself is badly wounded. He asks his armor bearer to finish him off, but the armor bearer refuses, out of respect for Saul. So Saul takes his own life. The Israelites are defeated and flee. And to make things even worse, the Philistines cut off Saul's head and attach his body to a wall for all to see. However, some of his loyal subjects come and take his body and those of his sons and give them a proper burial. What a tragic ending for this first king of Israel, who had so much potential. David, on the other hand, is victorious over the Amalekites and saves the lives of his family members. The contrast couldn't be sharper.

Think About . . .

We are advised often not to speak ill of the dead. Why is that?

Today's Scripture Passage
2 Samuel, Chapter 1

The Second Book of Samuel picks up where the first book left off, but the account the Amalekite gives of what happened to Saul is very different from what we just read in the final chapter of 1 Samuel. The most likely reason for the discrepancy is that the Amalekite is lying, hoping to gain favor from David for bringing the news that he killed Saul. It may well be that he came upon the dead Saul and took his crown and armlet. Because of his lack of respect for Saul, David has the Amalekite killed. The last part of the chapter contains David's lament over what happened to his king and to his best friend. There is genuine grief in David's moving tribute to these two men who have been so much a part of his life.

Think About . . .

David's expression of grief displays his skill as a poet and a musician. Why are poems and songs so often used at wakes and funerals?

Today's Scripture Passage
2 Samuel, Chapter 2

This chapter gets rather confusing as it progresses. What is noteworthy is this: David becomes king of the cities of Judah (the northern kingdom) and Ishbaal, Saul's son, becomes king of all of Israel (the southern kingdom). David asks the Lord what he should do, and God tells him to go to Hebron. He settles there with his wives, and the people of Judah anoint him king. Abner, the commander of Saul's army, appears to have considerable clout and makes Ishbaal king of Israel. Thus the stage is set for battle between Judah and Israel. Joab is one of the sons of David's sister, Zeruiah. In the next few chapters, the conflict between north and south plays itself out with scenes of revenge and bloodshed. All of this leads to David's eventually becoming king of a united north and south.

Think About . . .

Notice how often wars are fought between various factions within a nation. Why is civil war so hard on a nation and its people?

Today's Scripture Passage
Book of Jude

With only twenty-five verses, Jude is the shortest book of the Bible. You may not even have heard of it before. Not much is known about it either. It is clear, however, that the writer is upset with what is happening in some communities of believers. A few people seem to have caused a lot of problems by doing and saying all sorts of things that create division and lead people astray. Every Christian community, every church and parish, has to deal with individuals who put themselves first and think they are above the law. These people need to be dealt with so that the community does not end up destroying itself. Though the Book of Jude may seem rather negative in tone, verses 20–21 offer some great advice on how to stay on the right path. The book ends with a beautiful passage of praise to God.

Think About . . .

What is the best way to deal with difficult people within a community or organization?

Today's Scripture Passage
2 Samuel, Chapter 3

Verses 1 and 36 in this chapter are key verses regarding David. David's house grows stronger, and the people are pleased with everything he does. You may have been surprised by the listing of David's wives and offspring. By the end of the chapter, he gains back his first wife, Michal. Realize that it is common at this time for men, especially powerful men, to have several wives. This is one way of society's making sure all women are taken care of, as they have virtually no rights of their own. It is also a way of cementing political alliances, a common practice with monarchies throughout history. Also, note that even though Abner switches to David's side, he is still killed by Joab as an act of revenge. Even so, David remains innocent of bloodshed and actually shows deep respect for Abner. It seems David can do no wrong.

Think About . . .

Reflect on the qualities that make David such a good king.

Today's Scripture Passage
2 Samuel, Chapter 4

This is a rather gruesome story of Ishbaal's murder. With Abner gone, Ishbaal's confidence also disappears. The two brothers, Baanah and Rimmon, apparently think assassinating Ishbaal will put them in good standing with David because Ishbaal represents the last obstacle to David's becoming king of all of Israel. In a particularly ruthless manner, the brothers kill Ishbaal while he is taking a nap. They behead him and proudly present the head to David, who reacts just the way we have come to expect of this leader who is always so respectful of other kings: he is very upset and, just as with the Amalekite who reported he had killed Saul, David has the two men killed and treated as ruthlessly as they treated Ishbaal. Note that in verse 4, we learn that Jonathan has a son named Mephibosheth or Meribbaal who has a physical disability. He appears again in a few chapters.

Think About . . .

How do you show respect for those in authority? How could you improve in this area?

Today's Scripture Passage
2 Samuel, Chapter 5

With this chapter and its events, David secures his position as king of Judah and Israel. Several important points are raised. David is thirty years old when he begins his reign of forty years. He has several more children, including Solomon, who eventually will succeed him. He conquers Jerusalem and makes it the capital of his newly united kingdom. This is strategic because Jerusalem is a fortified city on a hill, so it is easy to defend. It also lies on the border between Israel and Judah, and because it belonged to the now defeated Jebusites, it is a neutral city, which makes it the ideal choice for a capital. From this point on, Jerusalem is known as the City of David. The Philistines try twice to attack David and both times are defeated. Verses 10 and 12 pretty well sum it up. David's reign becomes firmly established.

Think About . . .

Why is Jerusalem so sacred to Christians?

Today's Scripture Passage
2 Samuel, Chapter 6

By bringing the ark of the Covenant into Jerusalem, David makes Jerusalem the religious capital of his kingdom, as well as the political capital. The ark, as we know, is the holiest object in Judaism and has accompanied the people since they left Egypt. Because it is so holy, only those who are consecrated are allowed to touch it. This helps explain why Uzzah suffers death for touching the ark, even though he is merely trying to help. This reinforces the idea that the ark is sacred. David's famous dance before the ark in Jerusalem may strike us as rather extreme; after all, David is basically dancing in his underwear! Michal later criticizes him for it, but David simply saw this as the best way to celebrate his deep love for God.

Think About . . .

Could you see yourself worshiping God by dancing? Why or why not?

Today's Scripture Passage

2 Samuel, Chapter 7

The word *house* plays a pivotal role in this important chapter. In Hebrew the word can be used both for *temple* and *dynasty*. David desires to build a permanent house for God, and God responds by promising David an eternal house. This covenant that Nathan reveals to David is critical to salvation history. God is promising David that his line, unlike Saul's, will last forever. Later this promise will be linked to a messiah expected to come from the line of David. It is also revealed to David that his son will build a house for God, as indeed Solomon does during his reign. The Temple will then become the center of worship for the Jews. David responds in his typical way: by praying to God and giving God praise.

Think About . . .

Verse 22 is a beautiful mini-prayer to God. Repeat it a few times slowly. Let it be your prayer today.

Today's Scripture Passage
2 Samuel, Chapters 8–9

The Amtrak train that runs from Chicago to the Pacific Northwest is named the Empire Builder, after James J. Hill, the railroad tycoon. That name is apt for David in chapter 8. Slowly and steadily, he is building an empire in the Middle East, and verses 6 and 14 repeat a recurring theme: the Lord gives David victory wherever David goes. In chapter 9, David fulfills a promise he made to Jonathan in 1 Samuel, chapter 20. He gives Jonathan's son the land that belonged to his grandfather Saul. He also insists that Mephibosheth (in some Bible translations he is referred to as Meribbaal) always eat at his table, a great honor for this only son of Jonathan who is unable to walk. David seems only too happy to do what he can for the son of his best friend. Having a descendant of Saul at his table undoubtedly solidifies his position as king.

Think About . . .

Reflect on what it means to be a true friend to someone, no matter what.

Today's Scripture Passage

2 Samuel, Chapter 10

At times it does get a bit tedious reading about battles and commanders and warring groups. This chapter deals with the Ammonites and Arameans, both apparent threats to David's empire. When David sends envoys to Hanun, king of the Ammonites, the envoys are met with ridicule. By shaving off half of each man's beards and cutting off their garments halfway, Hanun makes them look ridiculous. This is a grave insult to David. The Ammonites, sensing they are in big trouble, hire the Arameans to help them. However, the Arameans quickly flee the scene of the battle when they encounter Joab. They are soon defeated and many of them are killed. The number of soldiers killed in battle is generally inflated to enhance the victory and the accomplishment. Now the only enemy left is the Ammonites. The struggle to defeat them is an integral part of the next episode.

Think About . . .

What is an appropriate response to being insulted and made fun of?

Today's Scripture Passage
2 Samuel, Chapter 11

At the height of David's success, he allows himself to give into a temptation, which proves he is all too human. The great king of Israel, who has many wives and children, spies a woman, Bathsheba, taking a bath and has her brought to him. We are given no insight into how Bathsheba feels about any of this, but we can imagine she would not refuse the king. And so the plot thickens. David and Bathsheba commit adultery, and when Bathsheba becomes pregnant with David's child, David quickly has her husband, Uriah, called home to be with her. However, Uriah proves himself a better man than David: during a holy war, a soldier is forbidden to have sexual relations, so he does not sleep with his wife. David gets desperate, and assigns Uriah to the front line, where he is killed. David then marries Bathsheba. David has certainly lost his way.

Think About . . .

Why is it so important to learn to control our sexual urges?

Today's Scripture Passage
Samuel, Chapter 12

Nathan cleverly confronts David by telling him a story. The story parallels what David has just done, but David is too caught up in the story to realize it. By condemning the man in the story, David condemns himself. When Nathan reveals this to him, David repents of his sin. However, as we know, the damage is done and cannot be undone. All actions have consequences. In verses 10–12, Nathan tells David that his action will unleash a wave of repercussions within his own house and family, and, as we shall soon see, this proves to be all too true. David is also told that his child will die. He pleads with God to not let it happen, but it does. However, a second son, Solomon, is born to Bathsheba and David. He becomes the next king of Israel.

Think About . . .

Even the king learns that his sinful acts have consequences. When have you learned this lesson?

Today's Scripture Passage
2 Samuel, Chapter 13

With the tragic events of this chapter, Nathan's prophecy plays itself out. Amnon, David's oldest son and heir to the throne, rapes his half-sister Tamar and then wants nothing to do with her. She goes to her brother Absalom, who is determined to take revenge. Amnon's actions are strikingly similar to David's: he allows himself to be ruled by lust and disregards the consequences. Two years pass before Absalom gets his revenge by murdering Amnon. Through all of this, David appears almost unable to act. These, of course, are all of his children, and Amnon and Absalom are in line for the throne. Absalom is now a fugitive, Tamar's life is ruined, and Amnon is dead. David's glory days come to a screeching halt. Now he must concern himself with what Absalom will do next.

Think About . . .

When have you done something to get even with someone for a harm done to you? Reflect on what effect that act has had on you.

Today's Scripture Passage
2 Samuel, Chapter 14

The main point of this somewhat confusing chapter is that David and Absalom reconcile. It takes two years, but it does happen, thanks to an intervention by Joab. Through the telling of another story, David is convinced to bring Absalom back to Jerusalem. However, they remain separated from each other. We learn that Absalom is very handsome and also that he has a thick head of hair. These details become important later on. Absalom and David finally meet, and Absalom prostrates himself before David with his face to the ground. His not looking at David indicates his total submission to his father. David in turn kisses Absalom, which signifies his forgiveness and acceptance. Whatever his faults, David does love his children. The reconciliation between father and son takes awhile, but it happens.

Think About . . .

Think about family members and relatives you know who do not get along. What can this do to a family?

Today's Scripture Passage
2 Samuel, Chapter 15

Over the next four years, Absalom steadily erodes support for David by undermining him, especially in the area of justice. One of the king's responsibilities is to hear cases and make rulings, as judges do today. Absalom waits before the gate and talks to the people, convincing them that he would do a much better job if he were king. He slowly wins over the people of Israel. He also forms a following and recruits a guard to serve him. Absalom goes to Hebron, and the rebellion against David grows as Absalom fans the flames. David then flees his city, Jerusalem, and tries to determine who is truly loyal to him as he plots his next step. Hushai, David's friend, willingly becomes his spy to find out what Absalom plans to do.

Think About . . .

What a contrast to David's early years as king! His own son is moving to overthrow him. What do you think is driving Absalom?

Today's Scripture Passage

2 Samuel, Chapter 16

Two key actions occur in this chapter, one by David and the other by Absalom. Shimei, from the house of Saul, curses David and throws stones at him, claiming David is getting what he deserves for what he did to Saul and his family. David's aide, Abishai, is ready to kill Shimei, but David stops him. He probably reasons that this man could simply be carrying out God's will. David feels that he is under a curse. So Shimei is allowed to protest. Following Ahithophel's advice, Absalom's action is to go into his father's harem. By doing this publicly, he is declaring himself king. He has usurped David's throne, and this action likely consolidates support from all the forces that are for Absalom and against David.

Think About . . .

Why do you think so many people support Absalom? Can you think of any modern-day parallels?

Today's Scripture Passage
2 Samuel, Chapter 17

It is safe to say that had Absalom followed the advice of Ahithophel, he most likely would have defeated David and taken a decisive step toward becoming the next king. However, he chooses to follow Hushai's advice. Why? There are several reasons, but mainly because Hushai appeals to Absalom's vanity: he urges Absalom to go into battle himself so he will emerge as the hero. In verse 14, the narrator of the story points out that the Lord also sways Absalom to ignore the better advice of Ahithophel. This is to emphasize that God is clearly on the side of David. Hushai reveals the plan to David, who is then prepared for the battle to come. Verse 23 reveals that Ahithophel later commits suicide because his advice is not acted upon. No doubt he also fears what David and his forces might do to him.

Think About . . .

How do you go about making a decision when you receive conflicting advice?

Today's Scripture Passage
2 Samuel, Chapter 18

David never ceases to amaze us with his human-ness. With the defeat and death of Absalom, he has every reason to be glad. After all, Absalom was a very serious threat to his kingship. But Absalom is David's son, and despite all he has done against his father, David still loves him. Even when David senses that his troops will most likely defeat Absalom, he still tells Joab to go easy on him. Joab does not follow David's advice, how-ever, and quickly kills Absalom, unlike the messen-ger who also had the opportunity but chose not to. The last verse of the chapter contains David's deeply moving words in regard to the news about his son. No matter what, Absalom was still his son. David has lost another son to violence.

Think About . . .

Reflect on how difficult it must be for a parent or guardian to lose a child. Does it make it any easier if they have not gotten along?

Today's Scripture Passage
2 Samuel, Chapter 19

A lot happens in this chapter, but a few points merit special attention. First of all, David's overwhelming grief for Absalom actually demoralizes the troops. Joab helps David snap out of it by persuading him that he is going to lose his men if he gives the appearance that they mean nothing to him. Second, David forgives Shimei, who hurled stones and insults at David in chapter 16. David also continues his generosity to Mephibosheth, Jonathan's son. Finally, at the end of the chapter, we learn about the tension between Israel (north) and Judah (south). This is a rather ominous sign of what lies ahead. David has worked hard to create a united kingdom, but the rivalry between north and south remains strong.

Think About . . .

Grief is a personal and yet universal emotion. Would you agree with Joab's statement that David is grieving too much? Is it possible to grieve too much?

Today's Scripture Passage
2 Samuel, Chapter 20

David faces another rebellion from the north. This time it is led by Sheba, who is from the Tribe of Benjamin, Saul's tribe. David appears more concerned about this uprising than he did of Absalom's, so the threat must be serious. He sends Joab to pursue Sheba. Amasa, who was Absalom's general, is to gather the tribes of Judah for a counterattack, but he proves disloyal, so Joab quickly finishes him off. Sheba gathers his troops in the city of Abel, and Joab's forces lay siege to Abel. This is when a wise woman appears, and to save her city, strikes a bargain with Joab. She offers to throw Sheba's head over the walls. This satisfies Joab, and the woman convinces the people of the wisdom of this, and so it happens. Sheba is dead, the city is saved, and the rebellion is crushed.

Think About . . .

Has humanity become any less brutal since David's time?

Today's Scripture Passage
2 Samuel, Chapter 21

As we move toward the end of David's reign, we encounter yet another story of revenge and sacrifice. This time it centers on the issue of a famine that strikes the land. David is told that because of what Saul did to the Gibeonites, something must be done to restore balance. So David goes to the Gibeonites to see what it will take. They tell him that seven of Saul's sons must be sacrificed. David is assured in his negotiations with them that nobody will have to die, but he doesn't read the fine print of the carefully worded contract before he agrees to its terms. The Gibeonites want to kill Saul's descendants themselves. It's a gruesome story. Let's face it . . . David is outsmarted here. He should have consulted with God before signing the contract. However, verse 14 tells us that, despite the troubling solution David agrees to, God responds by lifting the famine.

Think About . . .

David's continued respect for his predecessor, Saul, is noteworthy. How do we honor our dead?

Today's Scripture Passage
2 Samuel, Chapter 22

This song of thanksgiving by David sounds very
much like a psalm. In fact, it is nearly identical
to Psalm 18. The imagery and language is vivid
and powerful. The song focuses on two aspects
of David's story—his deliverance from his enemies
and his military victories. The key passages occur
in verses 21–25, which link David's faithfulness
and righteousness to his success. This is, as we
know, a common theme throughout the story of
David. The image of a rock and fortress prevails
and is a natural metaphor for a military leader
like David. The final verse reaffirms the promise of
an eternal dynasty for David and his descendants.
Find Psalm 18 and read through a few verses,
noting how similar they are to David's song.

Think About . . .

> What lines or images in the song do you
> find most appealing? Reflect on them, and
> then read through them slowly as part of your
> prayer today.

Today's Scripture Passage

2 Samuel, Chapters 23–24

These two chapters conclude the books of Samuel. They begin with the final words of David. Notice how they reiterate David's faithfulness and the everlasting covenant God has made with his house. Once again a natural disaster is attributed to God's anger, this time for David's military census. Perhaps this is seen as a lack of trust in God. We must remember that as the people of Israel get to know God better, their understanding of how God works in their lives grows and evolves as well. Here they are still at a rather basic relationship, thinking bad things happen to them because God is angry that they have sinned. What they do realize is that God is indeed involved in their lives. How God is involved is more complex to define.

Think About . . .

How has your understanding of how God acts in your life changed from when you were younger?

Today's Scripture Passage
Proverbs, Chapter 1

With the Book of Proverbs, we get a good taste
of wisdom literature. Verses 2–7 clearly spell out
the purpose of this book. The way of wisdom is
continually contrasted with the way of foolishness.
Many of the proverbs are directly addressed to
young people, so you should feel right at home
here. Verses 8–9 serve as good examples of the
kind of advice this book is full of: Listen to what
your dad and mom try to tell you; their advice will
serve you well. Sometimes we don't like to think
of our parents or other adults in our lives as being
wise, but the fact of the matter is that they definitely have more life experience than we do. And
believe it or not, they were once your age!

Think About . . .

Reflect on some advice you have received from
your parents or guardians recently. What did
they tell you and why? Does it seem like wise
advice?

Today's Scripture Passage
Proverbs, Chapter 2

The Book of Proverbs is attributed to King Solomon, David's son, just as the Book of Psalms is attributed to David. Most Scripture scholars agree that a variety of authors contributed to both of these books. Solomon had a reputation for wisdom, so it makes sense that the Book of Proverbs is attributed to him. The first eight verses of this chapter provide good advice about why wisdom is so valuable. One phrase that recurs often in this book is "fear of the Lord." It is important to get away from the idea that we should be afraid of God. It is actually a much deeper and richer concept than that. A better way to define "fear of the Lord" is as a deep awe and reverence toward God. Throughout the Book of Proverbs, you'll notice that the author often contrasts the way of the wise with the way of the foolish. Verses 21–22 serve as good examples of this.

Think About . . .

What does it mean to walk in the way of the good and the paths of the just?

Today's Scripture Passage
Proverbs, Chapter 3

Many people strive for wealth and security in their lives. Wouldn't it be nice to be rich, to have everything we need? Add to that security, knowing that we are safe and nothing bad can happen to us, and, well, this seems like the perfect recipe for a good life! But, of course, the writer of the advice in this chapter tells us about a different path. True wealth and true security have nothing to do with lots of money and a security system; rather, as verses 13–18 and 21–35 point out, the way of wisdom is the true and authentic path to wealth and security. Put your trust in God and continually seek wisdom, and then you will be a truly rich, secure person. Notice that the pronouns that replace the word *wisdom* are *her* and *she*. In the Bible, wisdom is generally referred to as female.

Think About . . .

What makes you feel secure? What are the true riches in your life right now?

Today's Scripture Passage
Proverbs, Chapter 4

The image that stands out in this chapter is that of the right path or road. There is talk of walking and running, and there is always the contrast with the way the wicked go. That road is to be avoided. Verses 18–19 are perhaps the most pointed, highlighting the difference between the way of light and the way of darkness. Imagine driving down a country road with no lights on. You're just asking for trouble! Imagine hiking in the woods at midnight without a flashlight. It makes more sense to just stop and settle in and wait for the light of dawn. It is dangerous and foolish to walk in the dark. And even when you walk in the light of day, it is important to look straight ahead and concentrate on where you are going. So it goes with our path in life. Let us not be distracted by everything we see along the way. It is important to stay focused.

Think About . . .

Think of your life as a path or road. Where are you headed? Are you on the right path?

Today's Scripture Passage
Proverbs, Chapter 5

It isn't hard to sum up the message of chapter 5: don't commit adultery. Though this chapter may strike us today as a bit sexist and one-sided, it is not difficult to apply the underlying lesson. It is really a warning about getting sexually involved with anyone besides the person you are married to. There is certainly a lot of temptation out there, and we live in a society that seems obsessed with sex. It is a powerful force in our lives, and we must be attentive to our desires. What was true three thousand years ago is just as true today. Let us not be seduced by all the messages and by people out there ready to take advantage of us. Our bodies and our sexuality are too precious for that.

Think About . . .

What proverb does our society seem to be telling us about sex? How does it compare with the message of our faith?

Today's Scripture Passage
Proverbs, Chapter 6

Ants are pretty amazing creatures. They often appear as uninvited guests at a picnic, and we generally consider them pests. But if you have ever taken time to watch them, you will notice how hard they work. They are legendary for transporting objects much heavier than they are. They often swarm together in colonies, and they have a well-earned reputation for being industrious. Verses 6–8 sing the praises of the lowly ant. The writer is impressed with how they store provisions for the winter. They are always planning ahead, as if by instinct. Perhaps you have never thought of the ant as a symbol of wisdom, but it does make a lot of sense. You never hear the expression "lazy as an ant," and for good reason. Let us ponder and learn from the wise ant, who always has the big picture in mind.

Think About . . .

What are you doing today to plan for your future? What steps can you take today to make it happen?

Today's Scripture Passage
Proverbs, Chapter 7

Once again we have a warning about the evils of adultery and being seduced by a "loose woman." It may help if we see the seductive woman as a strong temptation in life. For many people, that temptress is alcohol or drugs. Becoming addicted is very much like being seduced. At first it seems like harmless fun. After all, who's going to get hurt? We can stop at any point if we want to, right? And slowly, it happens. More and more, we crave the drug and its effects on us. More and more, we lose control. And pushers and sellers are only too happy to draw us in further. And so it goes, until we have become an addict. Then it becomes very, very difficult to stop, to kick the habit. Reread verses 24–27. They offer a very accurate description of the effects of addiction.

Think About . . .

What, besides alcohol, drugs, and sex, can lure you into becoming a victim of a harmful habit? Reflect on the remedy that is described in verses 1–4.

Today's Scripture Passage
Proverbs, Chapter 8

"Please allow me to introduce myself. I am Wisdom, and these are my gifts." Try to imagine these words being spoken as you read again the attributes of Wisdom as described in this chapter. Wisdom was brought forth by God at the beginning of Creation and was there beside God as the world was fashioned. Verses 30–31 speak of how God takes delight in Wisdom and how Wisdom is in turn delighted with the human race. There is so much positive energy described here. The final five verses repeat a familiar formula: pay attention to the way of wisdom and stay on the path. That will bring you life. Wisdom is better than jewels and is certainly more precious. Strive to be a wisdom millionaire, a collector of wise insights that will get you through life.

Think About . . .

What passage in this chapter resonates with you? Which words help you grasp the importance of wisdom in life's journey?

Today's Scripture Passage
Proverbs, Chapter 9

Right in the middle of this chapter is one of the most famous passages in the Book of Proverbs. A deep reverence and awe of the Lord is where wisdom starts, where insight begins. Again the contrast is made between wisdom and foolishness or folly. We have encountered the word *Sheol* a few times already. In fact, it occurs sixty-five times in the Old Testament, although it may not appear in the translation of the Bible you are using. It is a Hebrew word that signifies a place of despair where the dead wait for release. It lacks the clout of the word *hell*, but it is actually quite similar. The basic idea is that it is to be avoided at all costs. The way of the foolish and stupid leads to *Sheol*, which is not where most of us would prefer to spend eternity. If you strive for wisdom and insight, you can avoid such a fate.

Think About . . .

Does the fear of hell motivate you to be a better person? What should motivate you to be a better person?

Today's Scripture Passage
Proverbs, Chapter 10

The next part of the Book of Proverbs is simply
a listing of wise sayings that are not necessarily
related to one another, as they have been in the
previous chapters. All the verses have a parallel
structure. In each one, the wise or good person
is contrasted with the foolish or wicked person.
The first verse is a perfect example: it contrasts
the wise or smart child with the foolish or stupid
one. Wise children—we might say children who
use their heads—make their parents happy, while
foolish children—children who don't think things
through—cause their parents a lot of grief. Seems
like pretty sound advice even after all these years,
doesn't it? That's the beauty of so much of what is
written in this book; it is timeless.

Think About . . .

How would your parents or guardians charac-
terize you? Do they know you pretty well?

Today's Scripture Passage
Proverbs, Chapter 11

Verses 12–13 deal with a topic that affects every one of us in some way. Putting someone down or belittling someone is never a cool thing to do, yet we all do it. It is usually when we don't feel good about ourselves that we seem drawn to put down others. A truly wise or intelligent person knows when to keep her or his mouth shut. In the face of someone's being unfairly criticized, we are smart not to join in. We all know people who like to gossip. It seems to give them energy. It certainly gets them attention, even if it is only temporary. We quickly find out—sometimes with a lot of pain—who we can trust and who we cannot. Why get caught up in the whirlwind of belittling someone or gossiping about someone? Eventually we will become the targets. Prove yourself worthy of others' trust and know when to keep quiet.

Think About . . .

When have you talked badly about someone? Do you consider yourself trustworthy? Do others?

Today's Scripture Passage
Proverbs, Chapter 12

"Count to ten." Have you ever gotten this advice? People generally give it when a person is about to lose his or her temper. The wisdom behind it is that even ten seconds can help someone cool down and gain perspective. Verse 16 focuses on the issue of anger and insults. This proverb comes down clearly on the side of restraint. Acting out of anger can make people do or say things they later regret. Why not exercise a bit of self-control so you don't have to backtrack and apologize for something you said or try to make up for something you did? Anger management is really what this is about. Don't give in to anger, and don't react to insult. You only add fuel to the fire. Quench it with a more thoughtful approach.

Think About . . .

Where are you on the "anger scale"? Think about a time when you could have reacted more wisely to an insult or provocation.

Today's Scripture Passage
Proverbs, Chapter 13

"Spare the rod and spoil the child." This was a common expression until recent times. It is very similar to the advice expressed in verse 24. Today corporal punishment is generally frowned upon as a means of discipline. It is not permitted in schools. The danger, of course, is that a person in authority could easily get carried away while physically punishing a child; however, the spirit behind this proverb is worth heeding. Children and young people should be disciplined, and parents and guardians who fail to discipline their children actually do them harm in the long run. We all need to learn right from wrong, and when we do wrong, especially as children, we need to learn that there are consequences. Without discipline, there can be no order and no growth.

Think About . . .

Reflect on how you were and are disciplined by your parents or guardians. How will you discipline the young people in your care?

Today's Scripture Passage
Proverbs, Chapter 14

Throughout the Old Testament, God's people are advised to watch out for and take care of those who are poor. Verse 31 highlights that mission and amplifies it. Those who are kind to others in need are told that they actually give honor to God, while those who oppress people in need insult God. Now it is true that many of us do not actively oppress those who are less fortunate, but our society does have some policies and attitudes that seem to keep down those in need. Often wealth is gained at the expense of others. We are called, as followers of God, to look out for our brothers and sisters who are struggling, and certainly not to add to their oppression. We need to find out when and where people who are poor are being exploited.

Think About . . .

How can you do a better job of being kind to those in need? Where and how are those who are less fortunate oppressed in your city or town?

Today's Scripture Passage
Proverbs, Chapter 15

Many times people who take a service trip to an impoverished area, especially in the Third World, return and comment on how happy the people there seem to be, even though they have practically nothing. Verses 15–17 contrast poverty with wealth; it is those who don't have much besides a cheerful heart, a deep respect for God, or loving relationships that come out ahead. No real surprise there; but we often fall prey to the idea that advertisers shove down our throats every day: we need to have more to be truly happy. More of what? It doesn't matter. Just more. Somehow those with less seem better able to sort out their priorities. It's simple, really: love and happiness outweigh all the stuff we clutter our lives with.

Think About . . .

What means the most to you at this moment? Will you feel the same way five or ten years from now?

Today's Scripture Passage
Proverbs, Chapter 16

Verse 3 has a simple message that can really help us keep our priorities straight. Many Christians ask God's blessing before they begin a meal. Teachers in faith-based schools often begin class with a prayer. Why do we do this? It reminds us that everything we do, every action we undertake, every plan we make should be entrusted to the Lord. Jesus himself, before he launched his public ministry, spent forty days in the desert fasting and praying. He asked God's blessing on what he was about to do. Before he was arrested and put to death, he went to the garden at Gethsemane to pray. Jesus was showing us the way to begin whatever we are about to do. According to the writer of this proverb, if we ask God's help as we start something, we will be successful in carrying out our plans.

Think About . . .

Today strive to remember this proverb and put it to use. Ask for God's blessing as you begin each of your tasks today.

Today's Scripture Passage
Proverbs, Chapter 17

Family and friends are two blessings in our lives. At different times, however, one may be more important than the other. The proverb in verse 17 is an interesting one. The first part reminds us that a true friend will always love us, no matter what. The second part tells us that our relatives are born to share our hard times with us. Thankfully, many of us can turn to a loving parent or guardian when we are experiencing a tough time. Others of us turn to friends or other caring adults in our lives. It is often in times of loss or hardship that friends and family members pull together to help one another out. During the difficult and trying times in our lives, we really need to surround ourselves with people who love and care for us. We need one another for support and courage.

Think About . . .

Who has helped you get through a difficult time?

Today's Scripture Passage
Proverbs, Chapter 18

"Hang in there!" This is advice we often give to someone who is dealing with tough times. Verse 14 reminds us that the human spirit is a powerful thing; it can endure sickness and suffering. We have all witnessed people in all sorts of struggles carry on with inspiring faith and spirit. The second part of the proverb, however, warns us that a broken spirit is almost too much to bear. If we have been crushed by life and our spirit is crushed as well, we will have a hard time recovering. After all, our spirit determines how we approach life, how we enter into each day and its joys and trials. That is why we need to build one another up and not tear one another down. We need to feed one another's spirit with positive energy so we can indeed deal with all the challenges that will come our way.

Think About . . .

What can lead to a broken spirit? Think about someone whose spirit you can uplift today. Begin by praying for that person now.

Today's Scripture Passage
Proverbs, Chapter 19

"Thy will be done" is a very familiar phrase to all Christians. It is part of the Lord's Prayer and reminds us that in the end, it is God's will that prevails. Verse 21 speaks of the same truth. We may make all kinds of plans and schemes, but ultimately God is in charge and God's purpose will come to pass. That is what we pray for, after all, in the Lord's Prayer. At times we can get frustrated at how life is unfolding for us. Someone else may be getting all the breaks, while we don't seem to be getting any. But we need to keep the big picture in mind. God knows what God is doing, and God's purpose and plan will be carried out. We need to remember that as we try to figure out why certain things happen that seem unfair or unjust.

Think About . . .

Reflect on what you see as God's purpose for your life.

Today's Scripture Passage
Proverbs, Chapter 20

We live in a society that does not have much good to say about growing old. That is why the words of verse 29 are so surprising. So many people spend money to make sure their hair is any color but gray. They don't want to appear old. But the writer of the proverb praises the beauty of gray hair and lets us know that old people are to be admired as much as young people. Many people steer away from nursing homes and care facilities for the elderly. They'd simply rather not be around people who are in their final years. Perhaps they don't want to be reminded of their own fate. Many cultures revere the oldest among them for their wisdom. To have gray hair means that you have experienced much in life and have so much to share with others.

Think About . . .

Think about how good it is to be young, and make up your mind to visit someone who has gray hair. Ask that person to share the stories of when she or he was your age.

Today's Scripture Passage
Proverbs, Chapter 21

Verse 31 gives us the image of a horse prepared for battle. In our era of sophisticated defense equipment and technology, we may find it hard to relate to this image. The meaning of this proverb, however, goes much deeper than merely arming a horse for battle. The truth is that no matter how well we prepare to take on a task, the outcome is ultimately in God's hands. This verse is a humbling reminder that we are human beings, and though we may think we are in control of our lives, deep down, we know better. In the end, God is in charge. Yes, we need to be prepared for what life brings, but let's not fool ourselves into believing that we are the masters of our fate. We are asked time and time again to surrender to God's will for us.

Think About . . .

Reflect on times when you have been reminded that your life is ultimately in God's hands.

Today's Scripture Passage
Proverbs, Chapter 22

About halfway through this chapter, the structure of the proverb changes. In many versions of the Bible, the section that begins with verse 17 is entitled "Sayings of the Wise." The introduction (verses 17–21) states the purpose of this next section, which is not really any different from the rest of the book but is simply more focused, with thirty sayings that end with verse 22 of chapter 24. Think of them as a parent's words of advice to a son or daughter who is about to become an adult. The five teachings in this chapter deal with a variety of topics, but perhaps the most relevant is in verses 24–25. The message is that it is not a good idea to hang out with friends who are hotheaded and quick to get angry. You may end up becoming like them and getting into trouble because of it.

Think About . . .

Reflect on your own experience in light of verses 24–25. Have you ever had friends who fit this description? How did they affect you?

Today's Scripture Passage
Proverbs, Chapter 23

Wine was a very important part of biblical culture. We know that Jesus's first recorded miracle was changing water into wine at the wedding feast at Cana. Then at the Last Supper, he transformed wine into his blood. However, like anything else, wine can be abused, and in verses 29–35, we are warned against drinking too much. In biblical times, people drank too much and paid for it the next day. The same thing happens today. The writer describes how seductive wine can be, how it impairs our sense of judgment, and then how it can affect us physically. When we abuse alcohol, we might say and do things we wouldn't say or do ordinarily. The red eyes, the strange behavior, the hangover the next morning are all signs that we have abused alcohol. This is never a good thing, and this teaching advises us against it.

Think About . . .

Why is drinking too much such a problem in our society? Reflect on how you deal with the pressures surrounding alcohol.

Today's Scripture Passage
Proverbs, Chapter 24

A few more wise sayings are added to the previous thirty, starting at verse 23. One that has an easy application to today is verse 27. Although it uses rural imagery in speaking about fieldwork, which is how most people made a living in biblical times, its real message is still very applicable today: Don't attempt to build a house until you have the financing to back it up. Most people today cannot afford to simply build a new home from scratch. So, with the bank's help, a deal is struck. The idea is to work hard and save money so when the time comes to purchase a home, we are ready. We will have the financing and credit that will enable us to either build a new home or buy one. Obtaining a new home is a big step, so we need to be prepared.

Think About . . .

Are you in the habit of saving money each month, of setting aside funds to help you later on? Why is this a good, but difficult, practice?

Today's Scripture Passage
Proverbs, Chapter 25

Here we return to a listing of wise sayings attribut-ed to Solomon. One thing you may have noticed is the frequent use of similes, especially in verses 11–14 and 18–20. These similes reflect, in large part, the ordinary life of people. Verse 17 warns us of being too familiar. If we are always at our neighbors' house, eventually they may come to resent us. We may enjoy being there and enjoy visiting with them, but by our being there too much, they may grow tired of us, and then we be-come more of a bother or nuisance. Another old saying is "Familiarity breeds contempt." When we spend too much time with someone, we may begin to focus on all the things about him or her that bug us, and vice versa. We all want to be and have good neighbors. We also must respect one another's space and be sensitive to the needs and time of others.

Think About . . .

How can you be a good neighbor to others?

Today's Scripture Passage
Proverbs, Chapter 26

This chapter is filled with proverbs about fools and contains lots of vivid similes. Two verses in particular deserve attention. One is verse 12, which reminds us that those who think they are wise are actually more foolish than those who really are fools. This is a stark reminder of the need to be humble and to remember that we always have more to learn. Verse 27 serves as a strong reminder that when we create trouble for others, we will end up in trouble ourselves. Both images in verse 27 relate to actions we take to trap or harm others. Eventually we are the ones who end up getting trapped or harmed. When we plot to do something bad, we unleash a negative energy that will come back to haunt us. We must always remember to analyze our motives.

Think About . . .

Why should you be suspicious of a self-proclaimed wise person? Think about a time when you got caught in your own trap.

Today's Scripture Passage
Proverbs, Chapter 27

You know by now that there are several translations of the Bible. It is important to remember that
each version is an interpretation, because it is
impossible to accurately translate from one language to another. One word or phrase can be
translated in several different ways. A good example is verse 19. Here are three interpretations
of that verse: (1) New Revised Standard Version:
"Just as water reflects the face, / so one human
heart reflects another," (2) Good News translation: "It is your own face that you see reflected
in the water and it is your own self that you see
in your heart," (3) New American Bible: "As one
face differs from another, / so does one human
heart from another." The differences in meaning
provide a graphic example of the challenges of
translating accurately.

Think About . . .

Reread the three versions of verse 19. Perhaps
your Bible has a different version. Which one
speaks to you most clearly?

Today's Scripture Passage
Proverbs, Chapter 28

Luke's Gospel tells the familiar story of the forgiving father and the prodigal son (see chapter 15). The proverb in verse 19 seems to predict exactly what happens in the first part of the story. The younger son goes off in worthless pursuits and ends up spending all of his inheritance with absolutely nothing to show for it. He comes back home flat broke. The older brother who stayed behind has never known poverty, because he has worked the land and worked hard all his life. We know the parable is about more than poverty and wealth, but this proverb does remind us of the value of hard work. So many other things may seem more glamorous, especially get-rich-quick schemes we hear about or may even be lured into. In the end, though, it is an honest day's work that pays off.

Think About . . .

What would be your dream job? What meaningful work do you sense God calling you to?

Today's Scripture Passage
Proverbs, Chapter 29

The good and righteous leader will cause people to be happy. The wicked ruler will cause people to groan with unhappiness. Think about the world. We certainly see a variety of rulers, some good, some bad, most somewhere in between. Though we know it is impossible for a leader to please everyone, we know we can gauge the effectiveness of a leader by how people feel about him or her. In the United States, polls often indicate the approval rating of our president. This is a fairly good way to measure how people are feeling about the leadership of the nation. Though it is true that a leader can't always be doing things simply to remain popular, it is also true that a strong and wise leader will generally win the hearts of the people he or she is leading.

Think About . . .

What do you see as the top five qualities of a good leader? What current leader has those qualities?

Today's Scripture Passage
Proverbs, Chapter 30

Go ahead: pick a number, any number. Numbers are a big part of our life. We learn to count early on, at least up to ten. Think how often in life we number things to help keep track of them. Top-ten lists are always popular. Three is a widely used number, in everything from baseball to jokes. Verses 7–33 are known as numerical proverbs because several of them are centered on the numbers 2, 3, and 4. Verses 18–19 serve as a good example. Notice how many images focus on nature and our own sense of wonder. Like us, our biblical ancestors often used numbers as an aid to remembering and as a way to provide a sense of order.

Think About . . .

Look again at verse 18, and then write your own verse to follow it. What four things in life leave you in awe?

Today's Scripture Passage
Proverbs, Chapter 31

This final chapter of Proverbs has two distinct parts. The first is the teaching of the mother of an unknown king named Lemuel. She warns her son about sexual promiscuity and drunkenness, and then she urges him to speak out for those who are voiceless and powerless. The second part of the chapter describes the qualities of a good wife. One thing we miss in the English translations is that each verse would have begun with a word whose first letter was a successive letter of the alphabet. That would also have made the advice easier to remember. What is really being described here is the truly wise person, even though the proverb focuses on the duties of a woman in the culture of the time. This ends the Book of Proverbs, part of a tradition called wisdom literature. The next few books continue in this tradition. Later in the year, we will look more closely at the Book of Sirach.

Think About . . .

Which qualities in verses 10–31 seem appropriate for anyone, not just wives?

Today's Scripture Passage
1 Corinthians, Chapter 1

In about AD 50, Saint Paul established the first of many Christian communities throughout Asia Minor. One of the earliest was in Corinth, which is located in modern-day Greece. Corinth was a major seaport with a very diverse population, and it was also part of the Roman Empire. Paul spent about a year and a half establishing the Church in Corinth, and then he wrote several letters to that community on a variety of topics. The letters help us get very close to what Paul was thinking and how he helped form this early Christian community. One big issue that he tackles right after his greeting is the divisions within the Corinthian Church. In the Book of Proverbs, we read a lot about wisdom; here Paul seems to turn the tables by claiming that the wisdom of the world is actually foolishness to God. Verse 25 sums up Paul's point perfectly.

Think About . . .

Reflect on verses 3–8 and read them as if they were written directly to you. How does this make you feel?

Today's Scripture Passage
1 Corinthians, Chapter 2

Wisdom and words were very important to the Ancient Greeks. The Corinthians were part of that tradition. Often people were judged wise by the loftiness and eloquence of the speeches they made. In this section of his letter, Paul makes the case that earthly and godly wisdom are very different. At the beginning of the chapter, Paul points out that he proclaims the mystery of God in simple terms and with fear and trembling. Paul speaks of Jesus Christ crucified and how the Spirit of God is the force that gives power and courage. True wisdom, real wisdom, comes from God alone. No human can hope to truly grasp the mind of God. What we do have and know is the mind of Christ, who revealed God to us. So Paul wants the Corinthian Christians to change how they view wisdom. This is a spiritual gift that helps us understand the other gifts of God.

Think About . . .

What do you know in your heart about God?
What do you believe about God deep within?

Today's Scripture Passage
1 Corinthians, Chapter 3

A strong message for the Corinthian believers! Paul doesn't really mince words as he explains to them that they really are still babies in their faith. They have a long way to go. The proof is in the fact that there are divisions in the Church, as people side with either Paul or Apollos. Paul urges them to think bigger, to think with the mind of Christ. All of us belong to Christ, period. There should be no division. The mission is too important. It's so easy to get distracted by what often amounts to petty quarreling and personality conflicts; somewhere in all of that arguing, the mission, the purpose of a group, gets lost or forgotten. Paul repeats his teaching about human wisdom. There is no point in bragging about human leaders. We all belong to God.

Think About . . .

Verses 16–17 contain a beautiful teaching about how we ought to view ourselves. If we truly followed Paul's advice here, how would we treat one another?

Today's Scripture Passage

1 Corinthians, Chapter 4

One definitely gets the sense in this chapter that Paul regards the Corinthians as children. Like any good parent, he has to remind them about their behavior and urge them to shape up. There are two great lines in the chapter. In verse 1, Paul describes beautifully what we are called to be. Translations may vary a bit, but our role is to be servants of Christ and to be stewards or guardians of God's mysteries. Think about what that means. Each of us has a very important role to play as a follower of Christ. In verse 7, Paul asks the simple but profound question, What do you have that was not given to you? Think about that. What do we have in our lives that we have not received from God? This question helps all of us stay humble and mindful of whom we are.

Think About . . .

Take a moment to reflect on all the gifts in your life. Spend some time naming them and thanking God for them.

Today's Scripture Passage
1 Corinthians, Chapter 5

In this chapter, Paul shifts gears and addresses some specific issues that the community is struggling with. He addresses the subject of sexual immorality. He clearly states that the community has a role in dealing with fellow Christians who act immorally. We can't just sit by and let people do whatever they please. Being a follower of Christ has its responsibilities, and we owe it to one another to act in a way that helps people get back on track. Paul is careful to say that we do not have the right to judge someone outside our community. But we do have a responsibility to those with whom we worship and pray. The whole question really becomes one of standards. What are the standards that Christians need to be held to?

Think About . . .

As followers of Christ, what is our obligation to one another in the area of morality?

Today's Scripture Passage

1 Corinthians, Chapter 6

It is clear that Paul is trying to convince the Christians of Corinth that they are to live differently from others. He brings up lawsuits and urges believers to settle disputes among themselves rather than resorting to what we would call civil courts. Then he returns to the issue of sexual immorality, obviously a problem for this local community. He again emphasizes his temple metaphor to make the point that the body is sacred because the Spirit of God dwells there. That is another reason why sexual sin is such a problem—sex is meant to bring two people together as one, and God is part of that unity. Misuse of sex is a misuse of that connection with God. Our bodies should give glory to God, not the opposite.

Think About . . .

Why is it so important that you treat your body, and especially your sexuality, with reverence?

Today's Scripture Passage
1 Corinthians, Chapter 7

A lot is happening in this chapter. Paul believed that the Second Coming of Christ was very near, which accounts for some of his teaching in this chapter. Paul is also being very pastoral here; he is trying to apply Christ's teachings to particular situations and lifestyle choices. Perhaps verse 17 best sums up Paul's message. He counsels everyone to live out the life they have been given by God. In Paul's time, that would apply to local issues such as circumcision, slavery, and marital status. It may seem odd to us that Paul does not speak out against slavery, but that is not his point here. His message is that these issues really don't matter. What matters is how well we remain with God. All else is secondary.

Think About . . .

How does Paul's advice in verse 17 pertain to you at this point in your life?

Today's Scripture Passage

1 Corinthians, Chapter 8

The issue here of whether or not to eat food that is offered up to idols helps us see where Paul is coming from when he speaks of community. The problem is not that the food is somehow tainted if it is sacrificed to idols. Christians do not believe in those false gods, so eating the food doesn't matter. It is irrelevant. However, eating food that has been sacrificed to idols might scandalize someone new to the faith or someone whose faith is not strong. Then the issue becomes one of charity. Think about others before you act. We do not want to be a stumbling block for someone else. Be aware of those around you and what they might be thinking.

Think About . . .

How do you change your behavior when you are around young children? Why?

Today's Scripture Passage
1 Corinthians, Chapter 9

The famous image of the athlete in verses 24–27 fits our world well. The Corinthians, like most of the Greek world, prized athletics and sporting events. Paul's metaphor of the runner is one they can easily identify with. Perhaps you have heard the expression "Keep your eye on the prize." This is what Paul is talking about here, and in doing so, he is defending his own actions as a preacher and teacher. All that Paul does, he does for Christ and to bring others to Christ. That is what keeps him going, keeps him running. He denies himself a lot of things so he can be in top shape to run the race. It is what any dedicated athlete would do to win. The only difference is that the prize Paul is aiming for cannot be displayed on a shelf; it is the reward of eternal life with Christ.

Think About . . .

Reflect on an activity you are involved in that takes a lot of dedication. What have you had to give up to be part of this activity? Why do you stay with it?

Today's Scripture Passage

1 Corinthians, Chapter 10

This is a very rich chapter, full of memorable verses. Verses 12 and 24 both contain wise advice for all believers. Verses 16–17 offer a wonderful explanation of the Eucharist. But Paul's message in this chapter is perhaps best summed up in verse 31. If we always have the glory of God in mind as we set out to do something, how can we go wrong? Paul is a strong defender of the importance of conscience in making decisions, but he also emphasizes over and over again that we must always be mindful and considerate of others. Put others first, as verse 24 advises. Paul wants the new Christians of Corinth to be single minded in their actions and behavior: do everything for the glory of God. Always be conscious of others and what you can do to draw them closer to Christ.

Think About . . .

Spend some time reflecting on verses 12, 24, and 31. Which one seems most pertinent to you right now? Why?

Today's Scripture Passage
1 Corinthians, Chapter 11

Paul spends most of this chapter telling the community how they should worship together and celebrate the Lord's Supper. Paul reminds them about God's love and justices when they gather in their homes to talk about their faith, share a meal, and celebrate the Eucharist. At the time Paul is writing, no formal Gospels have yet been written, so the people share stories and certain prayers that the Apostles have passed on. It is clear from what Paul is saying to the Corinthians that a lot of abuses are happening. Some people are leaving the meal hungry; others are drunk. Some people are in a hurry or are not eating and drinking worthily with the community and Christ in mind. Because the Eucharist is at the core of Christian worship, these are serious abuses that need to be changed.

Think About . . .

How do you approach going to church? Are you focused on what is happening, or is your mind wandering all over the place?

Today's Scripture Passage
1 Corinthians, Chapter 12

Paul is at his best in this chapter and the next. He has come up with a brilliant analogy for the community of believers, one with which everyone can identify: the human body. He makes his point by highlighting various parts of the body and showing how each has a critical role to play in the proper functioning of the body. So it is with the Christian community. We can't all be great teachers or preachers, we can't all be prophets or miracle workers, we can't all have wisdom, and we can't all be healers. But each of us has a role to play. Not all roles are equal, but each of us is vital to the functioning of the community. In other words, we're all in this together.

Think About . . .

This is a good time to reflect on your gifts. What gifts do you have to help build the community?

Today's Scripture Passage
1 Corinthians, Chapter 13

Surely there is no more beautiful passage in the Bible about the primacy of love in Christian life. Paul delivers an eloquent message about priorities in life. It is so easy to get caught up in all the stuff that seems to be important to being a mature and respected human being. We can be the wisest, most selfless, most generous person on the face of the earth, but if we do not have love, then we have nothing. Faith is important, and so is hope. But love is what matters most of all, and it is what God is all about. Love comes from God, and if we live in love, we are rooted in God. It would be so good if the words of the song "They'll Know We Are Christians by Our Love" were true in the world.

Think About . . .

For verses 4–7, substitute your own name for the word *love*. How well do you measure up? Which qualities are the hardest for you to say about yourself?

Today's Scripture Passage
1 Corinthians, Chapter 14

The most controversial lines in this chapter are verses 34–36. Here Paul indicates that women are to be completely silent during worship. Yet a few chapters earlier (see 11:4–5), he clearly states that women can both pray and prophesy in church (as long as they are veiled). So what's going on? There are two possibilities. One is that Paul is simply being inconsistent. The second is that a later editor added this passage. The latter is the explanation many Scripture scholars favor. The early Church certainly had women in positions of leadership; that is evident in the Acts of the Apostles as well as in Paul's letters. Catholics believe that though the Bible is inspired, it is also a human document that often reflects the culture of the time, and that the Church helps us discern what is authentic to our faith and what is a reflection of life in biblical times.

Think About . . .

Why do you think Paul places such a premium on order during prayer and worship?

Today's Scripture Passage
1 Corinthians, Chapter 15

The Resurrection is clearly the focus of this chapter. Paul stresses that it is absolutely central to Christian faith. It is a core part of believing in Christ. Paul's wonderful counsel in the last verses sums up his message very well: Hang in there! Never doubt in the Resurrection of Jesus Christ, because all of us who truly believe will be raised up in Christ. We need to remember that as we strive to grow in our faith. Paul urges us to stand firmly and steadily, confident that God is on our side, that we will not have believed in vain. Paul admits that he is the least of the Apostles because he started out by persecuting the followers of Christ until his conversion. Verse 10 sums up the powerful role of grace in Paul's life and in our own.

Think About . . .

Reflect on the first part of verse 10. Say the words to yourself a few times. What role does grace play in your life?

Today's Scripture Passage
1 Corinthians, Chapter 16

The conclusion to the First Letter of Paul to the Christians of Corinth gives us great insight into the practical details of Paul's travels. He was the first great Christian missionary, traveling to all corners of the Mediterranean world. He seems tireless in his call to spread the Good News about Christ and salvation. Here he shares his travel plans and mentions several people by name, including names we also find in chapter 18 of the Acts of the Apostles, which describes Paul's visit to Corinth. It is striking how contemporary Paul's letter sounds to us—say hello to everyone, greetings from the other communities, and I send my love. Verse 13 is a great message of encouragement to the Corinthians and a reminder to do everything out of love.

Think About . . .

Think back over this First Letter of Paul to the Corinthians. What is the main message that stays with you?

Today's Scripture Passage
2 Corinthians, Chapter 1

The Second Letter of Paul to the Christians of Corinth differs from the first in some significant ways. It definitely does not flow as well as the first, which has led many Scripture scholars to conclude that it is actually several of Paul's letters combined into one. Nevertheless it is clear that the Corinthians continue to have some serious struggles and challenges within their community, and Paul wants very much to help them stay on track. In many ways, Paul seems most human in this letter as he responds to the various issues within the community, but he also has some very profound lines. All in all, this letter helps us catch a more personal glimpse of the early Church's greatest missionary.

Think About . . .

Keep in mind that Paul never met Jesus personally, that his understanding of Christ is a result of his conversion and prayer. Why do you think Paul seems to understand so well the mind of Christ?

Today's Scripture Passage

2 Corinthians, Chapter 2

In the last section of this chapter, Paul speaks of
fragrance and aroma. This image is easy for his
audience to understand because incense is often
used in worship. If you have ever been in church
when incense is used, you likely noticed how the
fragrance spreads throughout the worship space.
It permeates the air, and that is exactly what Paul
is comparing true believers to, especially in verse
15. The words *aroma* and *fragrance* both have
positive connotations, unlike other synonyms for
the word *smell*. Indeed, as followers of Christ, we
do not want to leave a stench or a stink behind
us. Those are things people want to get away
from. We want people to breathe deep and
inhale the good aroma of Christ's presence, to
want more. As Paul says, that fragrance can actually lead people from death to life.

Think About . . .

Reflect on how you can be the aroma of Christ
in the world.

Today's Scripture Passage
2 Corinthians, Chapter 3

When students apply for college, they need letters of recommendation that speak of their character and achievements. Naturally they will ask someone they know to write them a good recommendation. In verses 2–3, Paul uses this image to speak directly to the Corinthians, and all Christians, by calling us letters of Christ. Paul extends the metaphor, saying that we are letters not written with ink but rather with the Spirit of God, and not on tablets of paper but on human hearts. What beautiful images! Each of us is a letter written by Christ, a letter that anyone can read. At our best, we are positive letters of recommendation for living an authentic Christian life. Others will read us and want to be followers of Christ as well.

Think About . . .

Try to think of yourself as a letter of Christ. What do you express in this letter? What message do you convey by how you live and act?

Today's Scripture Passage
2 Corinthians, Chapter 4

Another vivid image appears in verse 7. Depending on the Bible translation you are using, the image is defined as an earthen vessel or a clay pot or jar. The clay jar might be the most helpful because we know that a clay jar is a fragile thing. But each jar or pot contains a hidden treasure. Paul has already endured a lot, and he is trying to encourage the Corinthians to persevere, as he as done. Our own weakness reminds us that our power, our protection, comes from God. We have to be careful with clay pots because they can break or get chipped quite easily. But what matters is the treasure inside each jar, the treasure that is the soul and essence of each of us, which transcends our physical being. In a sense, Paul is saying we can expect to be chipped and even broken, but our power to withstand the setbacks in life comes from God.

Think About . . .

Try to picture yourself as a clay pot formed and molded by God. What treasure lies within?

Today's Scripture Passage
2 Corinthians, Chapter 5

This is another rich chapter filled with memorable lines and images. Verse 7 states a simple but profound truth: "We walk by faith, not by sight" (NRSV). In a way, it is like saying faith requires us to walk blindly, not knowing for sure where we are or where we are going. As people of faith, we trust not ourselves, but God acting through us, walking with us. We simply cannot know all the answers or possess a detailed set of directions about where we are going. That doesn't require faith. Faith implies trust, which also implies putting ourselves in someone else's hands. If we are truly people of faith, we need to learn to trust that God is with us, walking beside us, and that walking by faith will get us where we need to be.

Think About . . .

What is something you are struggling with right now in your life? God is right by you, guiding you. Talk to God about your struggles.

Today's Scripture Passage
2 Corinthians, Chapter 6

Maybe later. Those are two words that don't seem to fit Paul's message very well. In the second part of verse 2, he states that now is the right time, today is the right day for salvation. Paul always seems to be in a hurry. And he actually is. He wants to spread the good news about Jesus Christ to as many people as possible, and he wants no one to block the way to salvation. It is not difficult to pick up the urgency in so much of what Paul says. He believes Christ will soon return, and there isn't a lot of time left. It's so easy to put things off, especially difficult or challenging things. And there are plenty of distractions that can keep us from getting to whatever tasks need to be done. No, Paul says, do it now!

Think About . . .

What are you putting off? What in your life, especially your spiritual life, needs to be tended to? Why not do it today?

Today's Scripture Passage
2 Corinthians, Chapter 7

In this chapter, Paul makes several references to Titus. Clearly Titus is an important figure in the early Church and plays a key role in Paul's missionary efforts, taking on the role of Paul's representative to the community. Paul is concerned about the Corinthians, and Titus's arrival seems to go a long way in alleviating some of his concerns. In verse 13, Paul expresses how relieved he feels when he gets a good report from Titus about his visit to Corinth. Paul obviously needs several associates he can trust: Timothy and Titus are two that are mentioned often.

Think About . . .

Try to imagine yourself sharing a meal with Paul and Titus as they talk over the growth and struggles of the early Christians.

Today's Scripture Passage

2 Corinthians, Chapter 8

In this chapter, Paul seems to be setting up a bit of a competition. He begins by mentioning how generous the churches of Macedonia have been, how despite being extremely poor, they have given abundantly. They have also given freely and way beyond their means. Paul sends Titus, with a couple associates ("brothers"), to Corinth, hoping the Corinthians will respond generously. He's implying, of course, that he hopes they can match or even surpass the generosity of the Macedonian Christians. We all know competition tends to bring out the best in people; it gives them a motivation to excel. Evidently the early Christians were no different. By Paul's letting the Corinthians know how generous the Macedonians have been, he hopes Titus and his coworkers can encourage a similar response from the Corinthians.

Think About . . .

How competitive are you? Does competing with others bring out the best or worst in you?

Today's Scripture Passage
2 Corinthians, Chapter 9

Paul continues in a similar vein to the previous chapter, talking about the collection for the Church. Verses 6–7 contain some beautiful advice about giving. First, Paul uses the metaphor of planting and harvesting to explain his point about giving. If you plant only a few seeds, you will harvest only a small crop. If, however, you plant a lot of seeds, you will have a rich harvest. It's the same way with giving to others. If you are stingy or tight, you probably won't receive a lot back. But if you give generously, you will be rewarded in kind. Paul also emphasizes that people shouldn't feel obliged to give, but rather should give what they think they can and should be cheerful about giving. Think about Ebenezer Scrooge after his conversion: that is the image Paul tells us God loves!

Think About . . .

How generous are you? How much do you give to the Church, to those in need, or to organizations that support those in need? Could you do more?

Today's Scripture Passage
2 Corinthians, Chapter 10

It is pretty clear in this chapter that Paul is defending his ministry, so we can assume he is facing a lot of criticism from some members of the Corinthian Church. His key message seems best summed up in the last two verses, which certainly can apply to us as well. If people are going to brag about themselves, they should brag in the Lord. Why would anyone brag or boast in the Lord? If we are truly in a faith relationship with God, we know we have little to brag about. As Paul says, people who think well of themselves don't really matter. What matters is whether the Lord thinks well of us. And really, what does anyone have to boast about? Pure and simple, God has made us what we are and has given us the talents we have. It's all God. We really have nothing to brag about; rather, we have a lot to be humble about.

Think About . . .

Why is boasting and bragging not very productive? What effect does it have on others? When is it appropriate?

Today's Scripture Passage
2 Corinthians, Chapter 11

In this chapter, Paul gives us some idea of all he has been through. In verses 23–33, he provides a list of all he has endured as a missionary for Christ. Life as the Church's first missionary is clearly no picnic! And Paul tries to make the same point he raised in the last chapter. If he is bragging, he is bragging about all that he has gone through, and yet he maintains that these things show his weakness, not his strength. It seems hard to believe that people would be critical of Paul after all he has suffered in the name of Jesus. But we all know enough about human nature to know that our egos so often get in the way, the message suddenly falling to second place because we want everyone to know how great we are. Paul is trying to do just the opposite.

Think About . . .

What is it that keeps Paul going? How does he or anyone who is suffering keep their spirits up?

Today's Scripture Passage
2 Corinthians, Chapter 12

Perhaps you have heard the Prayer of Saint Francis of Assisi, which ends with: "For it is in giving that we receive, / it is in pardoning that we are pardoned, / it is in dying that we are born to eternal life" (*Catholic Household Blessings and Prayers*, p. 124). Paul would add one more paradox: it is when we are the weakest that we are the strongest. In verse 7, Paul refers to a physical ailment he has to put up with. He has asked God to remove it several times, but he realizes that in this weakness, there is room for his true source of strength: God. Our flaws, our shortcomings, our weaknesses all give God some room to maneuver in our lives. They remind us that we are human and that God is God. This doesn't mean we should do nothing about a situation or ailment that can be dealt with or changed, but it does mean we have to learn the grace of acceptance at times.

Think About . . .

What do you see as your weaknesses? Take a moment to talk them over with God and to offer them to God.

Today's Scripture Passage
Jeremiah, Chapter 1

In some ways, Jeremiah is much like Paul. Together their writings are perhaps the most personal in the entire Bible, giving us a very good
idea of how human biblical people can be. With
Jeremiah, especially, we see the entire range of
emotions. It all starts here in chapter 1, with Jeremiah's famous call. In verse 5, God tells Jeremiah
that he was chosen even before he was formed
in his mother's womb. Of course Jeremiah has lots
of excuses: I don't know how to speak, and I'm
too young. God will have none of it and assures
Jeremiah that God will be with him through it all.
Every one of us has a call and a mission in life.
Jeremiah's is to be a prophet, which means he is
to be a spokesperson for God. As we shall see,
he is often ignored, put down, or even persecuted. It isn't easy being a prophet!

Think About . . .

Slowly read verses 4–8. Try to imagine God's
giving you the same message. How would you
respond? What would your excuses be?

Today's Scripture Passage
Jeremiah, Chapter 2

Jeremiah definitely gets right to the point. The message is simple: Repent! Several verses criticize the people for relying on themselves instead of God. Verse 28 is a good example. Jeremiah tells the people that they have been busy designing their own gods and have turned their backs on the real God. But when things get tough, to whom do they turn? Certainly not the gods they have fabricated. The people have forgotten about the God that led them out of slavery into freedom. It is time to turn back to God, to get back on the path to salvation. The image of the soap and the stain in verse 22 is typical of the kind of graphic images Jeremiah often uses. Scrubbing with soap won't wash away that guilt, says God. You need to repent.

Think About . . .

Why is it so important to be faithful through thick and thin? What is the true test of faith?

Today's Scripture Passage
Jeremiah, Chapter 3

As you probably noticed, this chapter has some pretty strong language. God is being compared to a husband who has been faithful to his wife. She, on the other hand, has betrayed her husband by being with several other men. Depending on the Bible translation you are using, the word *whore* or *prostitute* appears several times to make the point about how unfaithful the people have been toward God. As will happen many times in the Book of Jeremiah, such a graphic image and such vivid language serve to stress the prophet's point: the ever-faithful God has been betrayed and abandoned by God's people. Their infidelity and promiscuity show how far they have wandered from the Way of God. Keep in mind that the predominant image here is a broken marriage and that it is totally the wife's fault. This makes the point that God, the ever-faithful husband, has done nothing wrong.

Think About . . .

Why is the image of a broken marriage such a good one here?

Today's Scripture Passage
Jeremiah, Chapter 4

If it seems to you like this whole chapter is warning of an impending cosmic battle, you are right on track. That is exactly what the people are being warned about. The sense of a swirling, destructive force from the north and the feeling of doom are meant to provoke a reaction of repentance. If you have seen The Lord of the Rings film trilogy, especially the battle scenes, you get some sense of the picture Jeremiah is trying to portray for his listeners. God's message to the people is summed up in verse 18: You have no one to blame for this but yourselves. You brought this on. Now you will have to deal with the consequences. Not a very comforting message. We can begin to understand why Jeremiah is not eager to take on his vocation as a prophet. Talking of destruction and doom does not win you a lot of friends!

Think About . . .

Which of the many images in this chapter speaks the most forcefully to you?

Today's Scripture Passage

Jeremiah, Chapter 5

In verse 14, we are given a powerful image of the potential of Jeremiah's words. God tells him that his words shall be a fire, and the people are wood. When Jeremiah speaks, his words will devour them just as a windswept forest fire destroys everything in its path. It is important to note that people in biblical times believed that the spoken word was a living thing that had an energy all its own. To give someone your word was not taken lightly. Talk was not cheap in those days. It was often one person's word against another's. So when the image of spoken words being a consuming fire is used, it causes people to sit up and take notice. God assures Jeremiah that his words will have an impact.

Think About . . .

Reflect on how words can be like a destructive fire. What are some examples in your own life?

Today's Scripture Passage
Jeremiah, Chapter 6

Blushing is a very human reaction to shame or embarrassment. It is an involuntary facial reaction to either praise or criticism. Some of us blush more easily than others, which is what makes Jeremiah's statement in verse 15 that much more striking. He accuses the people, especially those in leadership positions (see verse 13), of acting in shameful ways—in other words, of doing things a person ought to be ashamed of. Yet they are not ashamed; they don't even know how to blush. Jeremiah is trying to explain how far off the track they have gone. Not only do they not feel a sense of shame for all the wrong they have done, but they are incapable of blushing. They have become so used to doing evil that they are hardened and have lost the very human capacity to blush. Once again Jeremiah has a way of making his point simply but effectively.

Think About . . .

What things cause you to blush? What things *should* cause you to blush?

Today's Scripture Passage
Jeremiah, Chapter 7

Jeremiah is summoned by the Lord to preach at the entrance to the Temple. This is, of course, the center of worship for the people, the great Temple built by David's son, Solomon. It is the dwelling place of God and is regarded by the people as a safe place. In verse 4, Jeremiah repeats the same phrase three times to echo how the people feel: this is the Lord's Temple. However, Jeremiah is telling the people that if they continue treating strangers, orphans, and widows unjustly and continue breaking the Commandments, they simply cannot expect to be safe in the Temple. If the Temple is God's dwelling place, so is each person. God must dwell in us all the time, especially when we are dealing with others. There must be a consistency in how we live and how we worship. It's an age-old struggle for believers.

Think About . . .

Why is it such a challenge to practice what we believe once we leave the doors of the church?

Today's Scripture Passage
Jeremiah, Chapter 8

Jeremiah makes frequent references to nature
and animals. Look at verses 7, 13, 16, and 17.
These are images people can easily identify with.
Fig trees are common in the Middle East. The reference to the various birds in verse 7 is about tim-
ing and instinct. They all seem to know when to
migrate, mate, and nest. No one has to tell them.
Somehow, even though we are told and given
warnings, we still don't react. The snorting and
neighing of the stallions and the release of poi-
sonous snakes are ominous images of impending
destruction. As is typical of the Book of Jeremiah,
a variety of images and metaphors make the
point that no one seems to be paying attention
to the warning that things are going to change
dramatically. It is just easier to pretend nothing is
going to happen.

Think About . . .

So often we are given signs as to what might
happen, but we ignore them. Why is that?

Today's Scripture Passage
Jeremiah, Chapter 9

In verses 23–24, Jeremiah speaks of boasting. He chooses three things people typically boast or brag about: wisdom, power, and wealth. The first, wisdom, is generally regarded as a virtue, a good thing. It is one of the seven gifts of the Holy Spirit. Our world, of course, values power and riches. We always seem to be captivated by the rich and powerful. Yet the only thing worth boasting about, insists Jeremiah, is understanding and knowing the Lord. And to know the Lord is to know that God acts with a constant love and always does what is just and right. In that God takes delight. That's a beautiful and reassuring idea. It's so easy for us to get caught up in ourselves or to believe that we really are special and in some way superior to others. God knows better. We should too.

Think About . . .

Try to focus on God's steadfast love. God loves you, no matter what. And God takes delight in all that is just and right. Do you?

Today's Scripture Passage
Jeremiah, Chapter 10

In Jeremiah's time, the worship of idols, or false
gods, was prevalent everywhere. The Jewish
people were the only people in the biblical world
who did not worship idols. They believed in
one true God who could not be captured in an
image. Statues and likenesses of Yahweh were
forbidden. Only with the coming of Christianity would there be depictions of the Trinity and
of Jesus, the Son of God. In the first part of this
chapter, Jeremiah makes fun of these fabricated
gods—carved from wood, decorated with silver
and gold, these gods can't even walk by themselves but have to be carried everywhere. In the
end, they are simply decorated pieces of wood
that have no real power. And yet the Chosen
People seem enthralled with these false gods all
around them. How sad when they have a truly
powerful God on their side!

Think About . . .

Why do you think the people of the time were
so fascinated with idols? Can you draw any
comparisons to our society today?

Today's Scripture Passage
Jeremiah, Chapter 11

In verses 18–20, Jeremiah voices his fears about his enemies. As a prophet who speaks the truth, he often says things people do not want to hear. Here Jeremiah speaks of his life being threatened. He compares himself to a gentle lamb being led off to slaughter, a common image in a land of sheep and shepherds. We can't help but draw comparisons to Jesus, who is often referred to as the Lamb of God. In fact, of all the Old Testament figures, Jeremiah seems the most like Christ. Jeremiah's enemies want to cut him down and remove all traces of his name from the earth. To not be remembered by anyone is considered a terrible fate, especially if you do not have children to carry on your name and memory. Jeremiah, like Jesus, did not marry.

Think About . . .

Why is someone who speaks the truth so threatening to people? Who in our society has suffered or died for speaking out against evil?

Today's Scripture Passage
Jeremiah, Chapter 12

In verses 1–6, we have the first of what are often referred to as the laments or confessions of Jeremiah. His first question to God is one that resounds through the ages: Why do the wicked prosper? This seems to Jeremiah, and perhaps to us, a gross injustice. It just isn't fair. It's not the way things are supposed to be. Good people should prosper, and bad people should get what's coming to them. God's response in verses 5–6 is not very reassuring. God tells Jeremiah that things will get worse before they get better. Even Jeremiah's own family and relatives will turn against him. So Jeremiah gets little comfort in his first question to God. What is striking here is how honest and forthright Jeremiah is in questioning God and sharing his doubts and fears. It shows that he has a very personal relationship with God.

Think About . . .

What questions do you want to ask of God right now? Go ahead and ask them.

Today's Scripture Passage
Jeremiah, Chapter 13

What is perhaps most striking in this chapter is the first image we are given. God tells Jeremiah to buy a linen loincloth, which serves as underwear for men. Why such a strange, unholy image? The point is in what God asks Jeremiah to do with the loincloth. He is to hide it in a hole in the rocks by the river, and so he does. When God tells him to retrieve it several days later, Jeremiah sees that the loincloth is ruined. God is giving Jeremiah and the people a graphic image of what is happening to them. God is as close to us as the clothing we wear on our bodies. But the people have distanced themselves from God. They have walked away from such a close relationship to God. And so, like the ruined loincloth, they have ruined their close connection to God.

Think About . . .

What image can you think in your life that would show a ruined relationship? What object could you use to make the kind of point Jeremiah is making?

Today's Scripture Passage
Jeremiah, Chapter 14

The beginning of this chapter describes the effect of a drought. It is easy to picture the scene. The ground is cracked, the wells are dry, and the animals are panting. It is a horrible thing to be without water. Those of us in the United States have never experienced this kind of drought. Clean water supplies might dwindle during emergencies, but there is at least water to be had. We can also boil and sterilize it to make it drinkable. But to have absolutely no water is hard to imagine. Water is a powerful symbol of life, especially for people in the dry climates of the Middle East. If water represents God's life and energy, what happens when it is gone? If people lose their thirst for God, what will happen to them?

Think About . . .

Imagine going without any water for three days. What would happen to your priorities in life?

Today's Scripture Passage
Jeremiah, Chapter 15

In verses 10–21, we learn about Jeremiah's second lament or confession. In verse 16, he uses eating as a metaphor for how he makes God's words part of himself. He describes the joy and delight he experiences in joining himself with God. It really is a lovely image. He acknowledges that God called him by name, as we recall from the first chapter. All that said, however, he still complains about how his pain is increasing and how his wounds are incurable. In some ways, he is speaking for the people as well, especially when they are in exile, far away from their homeland. In verses 19–21, we hear words from God that give hope: I am with you to deliver you from the clutches of the wicked. You will prevail. I am on your side. This is indeed a welcome message for a suffering people.

Think About . . .

Why is hope such an important thing? What happens when someone gives up hope?

Today's Scripture Passage
Jeremiah, Chapter 16

This chapter opens with the message that Jeremiah is to remain celibate, that he is not to marry or have children. The basic reason? There is just no point. The land and its inhabitants will be destroyed, so why marry and have children only to see them perish later? There is, however, a symbolic significance to Jeremiah's celibacy. As an unmarried man, which is highly unusual in Jewish society at this time, he stands as a symbol of Israel as well—isolated and alone. Granted, this paints a rather negative picture of celibacy, and it is not the reason most people choose celibacy today. We hope priests or religious women or men choose celibacy for more positive reasons—to be more available to serve God, for instance. But Jeremiah's prophetic role asks much of him, and in this case, his very life becomes a symbol.

Think About . . .

In what ways can celibacy be a positive choice for people?

Today's Scripture Passage
Jeremiah, Chapter 17

In verses 14–18, we encounter the third confession or lament of Jeremiah. This time, however, his tone is different. He asks God for help so he can be healed and saved. He mentions those who make fun of him, but he reminds God that he has stuck with it. He sees God as his refuge when times get rough, and he asks for protection in typical Old Testament style: let those who persecute me be disgraced, but don't let that happen to me. Bring bad things to them, but not me. In the New Testament, Jesus tells us to love our enemies and pray for our persecutors. This is a very different message from what Jeremiah prays for here. Jesus is calling us to a higher standard, to a very different way of looking at the world. Jeremiah does pray with a certain confidence in God that we haven't seen very much of.

Think About . . .

Time and time again, Jeremiah shows us his humanity. How is his prayer about his persecutors an understandable approach to take?

Today's Scripture Passage
Jeremiah, Chapter 18

If you have ever watched a potter working at the wheel fashioning a pot, you have an idea how one false or careless move can wreck the pot. A potter controls the shape, texture, and consistency of the pot, and an experienced potter can create a beautifully shaped pot by gently and subtly working the clay as it spins around. If a potter does not like how the pot is turning out, she or he can simply start over. We are like clay in God's hands, and God is free to shape us as God wills. This is not so much to show that God's actions are arbitrary, but rather that God is almighty. God is the Master potter at the wheel, making each of us distinct. It is impossible for a potter to fashion two identical pots. Similarly God has made each of us unique.

Think About . . .

Imagine yourself as clay being shaped by God's loving hands. Now try to imagine this as a lifelong process.

Today's Scripture Passage
Jeremiah, Chapter 19

Jeremiah is told to go and buy a clay jar and to take some of the priests and elders with him. Then, in their sight, he is to smash the jar in front of them. What is the point? The earthenware jug probably serves as a symbol of Jerusalem, and this important city, the site of the Temple, is going to be destroyed just like the jug. It is impossible to put a shattered pot back together. It is ruined. This certainly seems like an ominous message for Jerusalem. And the fact that Jeremiah does it in front of the Jewish leaders is also part of the message. They are responsible for what will happen. There is no doubt the end is near. The words and images seem to be building to a climax. Jerusalem's days are numbered.

Think About . . .

Try to picture Jeremiah with the elders and priests, delivering this somber message. How do you think they might react?

Today's Scripture Passage
Jeremiah, Chapter 20

If we had any doubt up to this point about how Jeremiah feels about being a prophet, there is no question after reading this chapter. In another of his confessions or laments, Jeremiah tells God he is simply fed up. He feels God has tricked him. He wants to quit being a prophet, and yet he can't help it; he has to speak out. But whenever he does, he gets made fun of. He even goes so far as to curse the very day he was born. He wishes he had died in his mother's womb! Those are strong words for a man of God. It almost makes us cringe to hear such brutal honesty expressed to God. And yet, because of this, we know how close Jeremiah is to God. Because of his deep commitment, Jeremiah can be completely honest with God. What a tribute to his deep, abiding faith!

Think About . . .

Have you ever tried to be really honest with God? Try it. And think about it: God knows everything about us—what can you say that would possibly shock God?

Today's Scripture Passage
Jeremiah, Chapter 21

Jeremiah lives in turbulent times. The power of Nebuchadnezzar, the king of Babylon, is growing steadily, and Jeremiah knows the king will soon destroy Jerusalem. During this period of Jeremiah's life, Zedekiah is king of Judah, and Jeremiah has little time for him. In turn, Zedekiah has Jeremiah beaten and imprisoned. With Babylon looming on the horizon, Jeremiah tries hard to warn the people to repent. He tries to tell them that all will soon be lost. No one wants to hear any of this doom and gloom, of course—least of all, the king, who often tries to silence this irritating prophet. You can almost hear Jeremiah saying, "Fine, don't believe me, but don't say I didn't warn you." Almost five hundred years later, Jesus makes a similar prophecy about Jerusalem, which is eventually destroyed by the Romans.

Think About . . .

Why is it so hard for people to be told to shape up? What in you resists that kind of message?

Today's Scripture Passage
Jeremiah, Chapter 22

Jeremiah's message to Jehoiakim, son of the good king Josiah, has a contemporary sound to it. Verse 13 rings through the ages as an accusation against all those who build their wealth and success unjustly, who oppress others so they can have what they want. Jehoiakim builds himself the best palace money can buy and pays his workers nothing. This corrupt king is contrasted with his righteous father, who was so good and generous to the poor. Jehoiakim seems to have just one thing on his mind—more of everything. Jeremiah also has one thing on his mind—convincing this self-absorbed king that his days are numbered. Our affluent society is filled with Jehoiakims who worship the god of gain and greed, always wanting something newer and flashier and better. It never ends. But Jeremiah can foresee the end, and it is not a pretty sight.

Think About . . .

If Jeremiah were a prophet today, what would his message be?

Today's Scripture Passage
Jeremiah, Chapter 23

In this chapter, Jeremiah goes after false prophets. There are many in the land, and they are false because they do not speak the true word of God, but rather they say what the people want to hear. Verses 16 and 17 are especially critical of these prophets who end up giving the people false hope. Of course, people would rather hear nice things that make them feel good and comfortable, but that is not prophecy; that is deception. Jeremiah refuses to lead the people astray, which is one of the reasons he is so unpopular. He is dedicated to telling it the way it is. For that he suffers. But he takes some comfort in knowing that God sees through these false prophets and that they will be dealt with, along with the priests. By deceiving the people, the false prophets are doing no one a favor.

Think About . . .

Who are the false prophets in our world today? What are their message and their approach?

Today's Scripture Passage
Jeremiah, Chapter 24

With this brief chapter about figs, the message is beginning to shift. We used to constantly hear about the need to repent. Now the focus is on two groups of survivors: those who were taken into captivity in Babylon (the exiles) and the others who either stayed in Judah or fled to Egypt. The two groups are compared to the two baskets of figs, one full of very tasty figs, the other full of inedible figs. God promises to be with the exiles and to accompany them when they return to their land. Again Jeremiah uses props to get his point across: yes, you are all survivors of a catastrophe, but some of you, especially all the cronies of the wicked king, Zedekiah, will ultimately fail. No one likes bad figs; therefore, they will probably be thrown out.

Think About . . .

Jesus also uses the technique of separation—one good group and one bad group. What other examples can you think of?

Today's Scripture Passage
Jeremiah, Chapter 25

For the first time in this long prophetic book, we encounter the number 70. One thing we need to understand about biblical numbers is that they are, more often than not, used symbolically. In our world, we tend to see numbers as very precise, each having a specific value. We have been trained that way, and we depend on the accuracy of numbers. In biblical times, however, numbers were often used to make a point. The numbers 7 and 12, for example, are often used because they represent perfection or completion. Think about how often they appear in the Bible and in religious language. Forty generally means a long time, and 70 represents the life cycle of an entire generation. So Jeremiah is saying that a whole generation of people will live their lives in captivity before being set free.

Think About . . .

Are any numbers symbolic in our society? How can numbers have power over us?

Today's Scripture Passage
Jeremiah, Chapter 26

This chapter marks the second half of the Book of Jeremiah, and the theme now shifts to a sort of seesaw between hope and blame. This part of the book is more of a history of what happens to Judah and how the survivors adjust to their new reality. Through it all, Jeremiah remains as the prophet of God and is continually reviled and scorned. In chapter 26, however, it seems that the people want to validate his role as a prophet. In verses 16–19, despite the desire of the priests and rival prophets to get rid of Jeremiah once and for all, the people speak up for Jeremiah and save his life. In contrast, another prophet, Uriah, is killed by orders of the king. Jeremiah does have a few friends in high places who look out for him, so he continues to prophesy.

Think About . . .

Why do you think Jeremiah is such a threat to the other prophets and to the priests? Why is his life spared?

Today's Scripture Passage
Jeremiah, Chapter 27

It seems like a rather unusual request. Jeremiah is told to put on a yoke. This is probably not an image we are familiar with, but it is familiar to people in biblical times. A yoke is a device made of wooden bars and leather bands attached to an ox, so that it can perform work, mainly pulling heavy objects, such as a millstone or a plow. Human beings do not ordinarily wear yokes. Jeremiah is to fashion one for himself and then tell all the kings captured by mighty Babylon that they are to submit to the rule of Nebuchadnezzar. In a sense, they are being yoked to the king and therefore controlled by him. Nations that refuse or listen to contrary messages from other prophets will perish. These are strong words from God.

Think About . . .

What image today might symbolize submission to someone else, as a yoke did in biblical times?

Today's Scripture Passage
Jeremiah, Chapter 28

Consider this chapter the "battle of the prophets." Hananiah challenges Jeremiah's prophecy of gloom and doom and says that within two years, Babylon will fall and all the exiles can return to their land. To prove his point, he takes Jeremiah's yoke and smashes it, as if to say, "Take that, Jeremiah!" Jeremiah goes away for a while, but he is soon given another yoke, this time of iron, to prove the point that all people shall be under the strict rule of Babylon. Jeremiah goes on to tell his rival, Hananiah, that he is a false prophet and that he has deceived the people and given them false hope. To top it off, he tells Hananiah that he shall die within the year. And, indeed, that is what happens. Once again Jeremiah is vindicated.

Think About . . .

There is always more than one voice on a controversial religious issue. How do you know which voice truly reflects the will of God?

Today's Scripture Passage
Jeremiah, Chapter 29

This letter to the exiles in Babylon is mostly a letter of comfort and promise. The core of the message is verses 11–14. This is one of the loveliest passages in the Book of Jeremiah. Even though the words are addressed to the exiles, they seem to jump off the page, and suddenly it seems like God is talking directly to each one of us. Reread these verses and start by saying your name as part of the message. The words of God delivered through Jeremiah are so consoling and inspiring. God reassures us that there is a plan for each of us, and it is a plan that leads to good. The passage reminds us of Jesus's words: that those who ask receive, those who seek find, and for those who knock, the door shall be opened. If we seek God with all our heart, we will find God there with us. Who could ask for more?

Think About . . .

Let verses 11–14 be your prayer. Say the words slowly and reflectively. Let the power of the words linger in your heart.

Today's Scripture Passage
Jeremiah, Chapter 30

A tone of hope certainly echoes through this chapter. Verse 19 even speaks of singing and laughing. We haven't heard much of that in the Book of Jeremiah. It is a message of consolation, as if to say, "This too will pass." These are words we all need to hear at various times. Sometimes we encounter tragedy and loss, and it feels as if our whole world is caving in. We can only imagine the sense of loss experienced by the people who have been exiled from their homes and held captive in a foreign place with no end in sight. Eventually God tells them, and us, that all shall be restored. Things will get back to normal. It will never be the same, but it will get better. Singing and laughing are always good and healthy signs. Hope is what we cling to in the rough times. The promise of better times ahead is what keeps us going.

Think About . . .

Who can you think of that always seems filled with hope, despite lots of difficulties and challenges? Pray for that person right now.

Today's Scripture Passage
Jeremiah, Chapter 31

Here we encounter another beautiful passage in the Book of Jeremiah. Verses 31–34 speak of a New Covenant. This Covenant, what we know as the Ten Commandments, comes from Mount Sinai and is summarized on the famous stone tablets that Moses brings down from his encounter with God. The Covenant God makes with the people is what keeps them going through all the centuries that follow. Now God promises a New Covenant that will be etched not on stone but on each person's heart. In other words, this New Covenant will be internalized, will be part of each person. It is a sign of maturing in faith when the rules and laws we learn eventually become just part of the fabric of who we are. That is the covenant God desires with us—one planted deep within, not just listed as a bunch of rules. Rules are designed mainly to provide guidance and structure. A covenant is a much deeper and personal commitment.

Think About . . .

Try to imagine God writing a message deep within your soul. What is the message?

Today's Scripture Passage
Jeremiah, Chapter 32

Investing in land is almost always a good idea.
In verses 6–25, Jeremiah talks about land he
purchases from his cousin. There is talk of deeds
and titles, similar to real estate transactions today.
The striking thing about Jeremiah's action is that
he does it when Judah is being ravaged by the
Babylonians. Everyone is preparing to flee the
city. No one is buying land or investing in real
estate—no one but Jeremiah, at God's instruction. Why? Because eventually the land will be
restored to the people, and life as they knew it
will be restored. So this is a sign of faith in God's
promises and a symbol of hope that what has
been promised to the exiles will be fulfilled. How
better to show confidence in a brighter future than
by investing in land in the midst of a crisis?

Think About . . .

How do the people who love you show that
they believe in you and have confidence in
you? What are the signs of their belief in
you?

Today's Scripture Passage
Jeremiah, Chapter 33

This chapter is about the restoration of Jerusalem. We are reminded in the first verse that Jeremiah is being held prisoner. He receives a prophecy now that is very different from so many before it. It is a message of hope for the people. It is almost as if God has a change of heart. God now promises to treat the wounds of the city of Jerusalem and to heal the people and show them an abundant peace and security. These are indeed comforting words for a people suffering exile. God says that all will be forgiven, and Jerusalem will be God's pride and joy before all the earth. The people will be showered with good things. At times it may be challenging for us to understand that the Old Testament reveals an ever-growing awareness of who God is and a slow movement toward a mature understanding of this God who gradually reveals himself to the people he has chosen.

Think About . . .

How has your concept of God changed as you have grown?

Today's Scripture Passage
Jeremiah, Chapter 34

Breaking a promise is a serious thing. It violates a trust and damages a relationship. So it is here in chapter 34. As Jerusalem is being attacked by Babylon, the king issues an edict that frees all the slaves. This is in accordance with the law that Hebrew slaves are not to serve longer than six years (see Deuteronomy 15:12–15). The people follow the edict, but then later they force the freed slaves back into service. This is a direct violation of the law, and God will not stand for this injustice. In verse 17, God gives the people the same medicine they dealt to their slaves. Because the people did not obey, they are also free now—that is, free for the sword, famine, and pestilence, all the horrible things that come with war and defeat. Disobedience has its consequences.

Think About . . .

What does it mean to be free? Does it mean having no responsibilities? or more responsibilities?

Today's Scripture Passage
Jeremiah, Chapter 35

The Rechabites believe that to be true to God, they must remain as they were when God first called Abraham. During this time, people are nomads, with no single place to call home except the inside of a tent. The Rechabites live a nomadic lifestyle, and therefore do not plant or harvest crops. Rechab's son, Jonadab, also forbids the drinking of wine, which explains why the Rechabites refuse the wine Jeremiah offers them. They are noteworthy for remaining true to their call. It is this kind of single-minded faithfulness to their ideals that God so admires. It is such a contrast to the rest of the Chosen People who seem to do everything except what is asked of them as followers of God.

Think About . . .

You probably know people who follow convictions that you don't necessarily agree with. Whom do you know like that? How do you generally react to such people?

Today's Scripture Passage
Jeremiah, Chapter 36

This chapter introduces us to Baruch, who serves as the scribe, or writer, of Jeremiah's prophecies. Think of him as Jeremiah's secretary and, at times, spokesperson. In biblical times, all writing was done on scrolls. The Hebrew Scriptures used by Jews in worship are still kept on scrolls. Eventually the scroll with Jeremiah's writings is read to the king, who has it cut apart and thrown into the fire. Obviously he is not too thrilled with Jeremiah's prophecies! He wants Jeremiah and Baruch arrested, but they are in hiding. Baruch then completes a new scroll. The point of this is that even though the written words are destroyed, they are still potent and will be fulfilled. Burning them will not destroy the truth of the message.

Think About . . .

Many people commit Bible passages and poems to memory. What Bible passages or poems do you know by heart?

Today's Scripture Passage
Jeremiah, Chapter 37

In this chapter, Jeremiah is thrown into an un-
derground dungeon where he is kept for a long
time. At one point, King Zedekiah asks to see
Jeremiah to find out if he has a message from
God. Jeremiah does, and he proceeds to tell the
king that he will be handed over to the king of
Babylon. Jeremiah then asks Zedekiah why he
is being imprisoned when he is simply telling the
truth. Where are the other prophets who said that
Babylon would not attack or defeat Jerusalem?
Jeremiah asks not to be returned to the dungeon.
In response the king keeps Jeremiah imprisoned
but now confines him to the quarters of the guard,
where he receives a loaf of bread each day.

Think About . . .

Take a moment to imagine what your imprisoned brothers and sisters are going through.
Say a prayer for them.

Today's Scripture Passage
Jeremiah, Chapter 38

As if being imprisoned for no other reason than telling the truth isn't bad enough, now Jeremiah is thrown into a cistern. A cistern is an underground container for rainwater. Luckily the one Jeremiah is thrown into has no water, so he is not in danger of drowning. But the cistern is muddy, and Jeremiah sinks into it. He will not last long there without food, so, at the request of one of the courtiers, the king orders him removed from the cistern and placed back under the palace guard. So much of what happens to Jeremiah can have meaning for us if we look at it metaphorically. Let's hope that none of us ends up being thrown into a muddy cistern; nevertheless we all have times when we may feel that we have been. But just as Jeremiah is rescued, we will be as well.

Think About . . .

Think about a time when you've felt like Jeremiah. What happened next?

Today's Scripture Passage
Jeremiah, Chapter 39

And so the dreaded event comes to pass, just as Jeremiah prophesied. When Zedekiah realizes the city is about to fall, he flees by night with his warriors. However, he is captured and must look on as his sons are killed, along with all the nobles who fled with him. He is then blinded and led off in chains to Babylon. Zedekiah's actual blindness only serves to highlight his spiritual and moral blindness. He refused to follow God's direction given through Jeremiah. Now he has lost it all. The tables are turned as Jeremiah, who was imprisoned, is now set free. Most of the people are taken off to Babylon; only those who are poor are left behind. Jeremiah, true to form, chooses to stay with his people. Thus begins the long captivity of the people in Babylon. It will last almost fifty years, until 538 BC, when Cyrus of Persia conquers Babylon.

Think About . . .

How can you be blind to reality or truth? What can open your eyes?

Today's Scripture Passage
Jeremiah, Chapter 40

As the events in chapter 40 unfold, we realize that there are now two groups: those in captivity in Babylon and those left behind in Judah. When Gedaliah is appointed overseer of the land of Judah, people scattered in other lands, such as Moab, Edom, and the land of the Ammonites, return to the land of Judah. With a slightly different account than in chapter 39 of the events following the conquest of Jerusalem, this chapter repeats the news that Jeremiah has decided to stay with what is called the remnant, those who remain in Judah. As you can imagine, life will be very different for this group compared to the exiles in Babylon. Remember that Jeremiah is given the choice. Clearly the exiles could also benefit from his presence among them.

Think About . . .

Why do you think Jeremiah chooses to stay with the people in Judah?

Today's Scripture Passage
Jeremiah, Chapter 41

This chapter is filled with chaos and brutality, and almost all of it is due to Ishmael. He kills Gedaliah, the king of Babylon's chosen leader, and also kills all the soldiers with him as well as the Chaldean soldiers. As if that isn't enough, he lures a group of eighty pilgrims on their way to the Lord's house inside the city walls and has them slaughtered and thrown into a sacred cistern. This holy place is now filled with bloody corpses, a desecration of a holy site. The only ones spared are those with some goods stored away. Ishmael's ruthless and self-serving actions are in direct violation of God's will that the people submit to Babylon. The result is so much bloodshed. It is almost as if cruelty becomes an addiction that eventually destroys those who inflict it so casually.

Think About . . .

Why is it easy for some people to treat others so inhumanely? What purpose does it serve?

Today's Scripture Passage
Jeremiah, Chapter 42

The remnants who have survived Ishmael's cruelty are ready to flee to Egypt. They want to go where it will be safe and peaceful. They ask Jeremiah for advice, and he returns to them with the message that God wants them to stay where they are. In fact, if they do flee to Egypt, trouble and misery will follow them. They are to stay put, and if they do, they will be built up. They are not to fear the king of Babylon. It may seem like strange advice when all the people want is peace and quiet, but that's the point. They won't find it anywhere but where they are. God will be with them, just as God is with the exiles in Babylon. The trick is they have to stay where they are. If they do, they will prosper. So often we are tempted to escape from an unpleasant situation. The lesson here is that sometimes God reveals to us the need to stay put and face the challenges ahead. Other times God calls us to walk away.

Think About . . .

Recall a time when you were tempted to run away from a messy situation. What happened?

Today's Scripture Passage
Jeremiah, Chapter 43

Despite all that has happened and the fact that Jeremiah's prophecies have all come to pass, the leaders, led by Johanan, refuse to accept Jeremiah's words. In fact, they accuse him of lying to them and accuse Baruch of convincing Jeremiah to go against them. And so, despite God's wishes, the leaders of the remnant force everyone to go with them to Egypt. This includes Jeremiah and Baruch. So now, despite his desire to stay in Judah with the people, Jeremiah goes into exile in the land of Egypt. How utterly discouraging this must have been for this holy man who has been through so much. Once again the people ignore the very thing they wanted to know—what God wills of them. Clearly they heard a message they did not want to hear. They turn away from God yet again and are now refugees in the land of the pharaohs.

Think About . . .

What is it in human nature that causes us to sometimes choose the very thing we are warned against?

Today's Scripture Passage
Jeremiah, Chapter 44

This chapter focuses on the sin of idolatry. Worshiping false gods is a direct violation of the First Commandment. In no uncertain terms, Jeremiah warns the people in Egypt that they are offending God by worshiping idols, and that the consequence of their sin is their not surviving in Egypt. They will never return to Judah. The response Jeremiah receives is as strong and definite as the prophecy he delivers: We will not listen to your message. We will continue to burn incense to the queen of heaven and pour out wine offerings to her. The people attribute their well-being to this practice and they refuse to give it up, especially the women. What can Jeremiah say? Very well, do what you want, but remember that you have been warned. You have chosen to deliberately go against the will and commandment of God.

Think About . . .

Why do you think the people react so negatively to Jeremiah's message?

Today's Scripture Passage
Jeremiah, Chapter 45

This short chapter in the long Book of Jeremiah contains an important message for Baruch, Jeremiah's faithful scribe. Recall that Baruch had to rewrite the prophecies of Jeremiah after Zedekiah destroyed the first scroll. In writing both scrolls, Baruch surely found the prophecies very discouraging. In one sense, Jeremiah's message to Baruch is sobering and humbling: He will not achieve greatness. He will not be Jeremiah's successor. However, Baruch is also assured that despite all the bad things that will befall the people, he will be spared. He will remain alive, and that is the gift he must cherish. Jeremiah's death is not recorded in the Bible, but it is generally believed that his own people killed him in Egypt. Baruch will live to ensure that Jeremiah's prophecies and story survive.

Think About . . .

Think of people for whom the gift of simply staying alive, of surviving, would be very good news.

Today's Scripture Passage
Jeremiah, Chapter 46

The next six chapters are generally referred to as "The Oracles Against the Nations." They are similar to chapters 13–23 in the Book of Isaiah, which appears right before the Book of Jeremiah. An oracle is a communication from God on some point. In Greek mythology, Delphi was famous for its oracles. Here, of course, as the title of the section implies, each of the oracles is directed at one of the neighboring nations. The first is mighty Egypt. Verses 17–24 capture well the spirit of the oracle: let Pharaoh know that his nation is doomed. It will fall and be disgraced. Verse 20 reveals that the conqueror will come from the north. This refers to Babylon. In verses 27–28, the remnant is reassured that they will eventually be restored to their land.

Think About . . .

What do you think God would say to our nation in an oracle?

Today's Scripture Passage
Jeremiah, Chapter 47

The metaphor in this oracle against the Philistines is that of a tsunami. The waters surge over everything and destroy it. The devastating flood refers once again to mighty Babylon. The image then switches to the sound of thundering horse hooves and the rumbling of chariots' advancing. It is the sound of impending doom. In verses 6–7, we hear the words of the Philistines, who plead that the Lord's avenging sword be returned to its sheath, but they realize that will not happen until God's will has been carried out. We might be struck by the fact that each oracle portrays an almost ruthless, avenging face of God. Nothing seems able to stop God's wrath against the nations. Again this image of God seems so different from the image Jesus reveals. Keep in mind that these oracles are not really directed to specific nations, but are meant to reassure the remnant that God will save them in time.

Think About . . .

Why is it not helpful to view a natural disaster as a message or punishment from God?

Today's Scripture Passage
Jeremiah, Chapter 48

The nation of Moab was one of the Israelites' old-est and bitterest enemies, which perhaps accounts for the considerable length of this oracle. The god of Moab is named Chemosh. You probably noticed several references to wine in this oracle. Moab is well known for its vineyards and wine presses, so that becomes much of the focus of the imagery here. The nation becomes a wasteland, the wine is drained from its vats, and all the pride of this great nation disappears, as its god and leaders flee before the conqueror Babylon. The last verse is rather interesting. Here, despite all the rhetoric of destruction and devastation, God promises better days ahead for Moab. Histori-cally, Moab was conquered by Babylon in 582 BC, five years after the destruction of Jerusalem. Moab did survive.

Think About . . .

Despite the worst that can befall a city or na-tion, it can and will survive. What are some recent examples?

Today's Scripture Passage
Jeremiah, Chapter 50

Now the tables turn on mighty Babylon. It may seem strange that after Babylon has been used to accomplish God's will, it will now meet the same fate. Some Scripture scholars believe these chapters were written after the fall of Babylon and thus have become the final oracle and by far the most extensive. Notice the list of entities mentioned in each verse following the phrase "a sword against" or "death upon," depending on the translation. We encounter the word *Chaldeans* many times; this is the name of the dynasty that is ruling Babylon at the time. Soothsayers or diviners are those who claim to see the future; both words have a more negative connotation than the word *prophet*. Every kingdom has treasures that would be equivalent to money today. In short, Babylon will lose it all.

Think About . . .

Try to imagine the map of North America someday divided into ten countries instead of three. Could it happen?

Today's Scripture Passage
Jeremiah, Chapter 51

Wait, didn't we just read this chapter? If it feels like chapter 51 pretty much repeats chapter 50, it does. There isn't much new revealed here, just some different images. It is also the longest chapter in the Book of Jeremiah. It's almost as if Jeremiah just can't think of enough ways to get across the idea that Babylon's number will soon be up. The chapter ends with another symbolic action that Jeremiah is so famous for. Jeremiah tells Seraiah to read aloud all the words he has written against Babylon and then tie the scroll to a stone and throw it into the famous Euphrates River. Seraiah is then to point out that this will also happen to Babylon. And stones do not rise to the top again, so Babylon's fate is sealed.

Think About . . .

The bigger they are, the harder they fall. This seems to be the implied message in the oracle against Babylon. Can you think of other examples where that saying seems to apply?

Today's Scripture Passage
Jeremiah, Chapter 52

The Book of Jeremiah ends with a recap of what has happened during Jeremiah's life. Curiously enough, however, no mention is made of either Jeremiah or God. Much of this chapter is also a repetition of 2 Kings 24:18–25. Look back at verse 10 of chapter 1: Jeremiah is given his call and is told that he will be set over nations and kingdoms, to root up and tear down, to destroy and demolish, to build and plant. That pretty much sums up what Jeremiah has indeed accomplished in his difficult life as a prophet. The chapter validates Jeremiah's prophecies and ends with the story of how Jehoiachin, king of Judah and a captive, is invited to dine with the king of Babylon and is given a daily allowance. That is a hopeful note for a prophetic book that is filled with gloom, doom, and destruction.

Think About . . .

Whom would you say are contemporary prophets? Have any of their messages or prophecies been fulfilled?

Today's Scripture Passage

Acts of the Apostles, Chapter 1

The Gospel of Luke is the story of Christ, and the Acts of the Apostles is the story of the early Church. It begins right where Luke's Gospel leaves off—the Ascension. By the end of the book, we will have traveled with Paul "to the ends of the earth," at least the earth known to the Mediterranean world. The central figures are Peter, Paul, and the Holy Spirit. The theme is clear: Jesus came to save everyone, not just the Jews, the Chosen People. This changes everything. In the Acts of the Apostles, Saint Paul travels from Jerusalem to Athens to Rome, and lots of places in between, to spread the Good News.

Think About . . .

Why do you think the author of Luke felt the need to write this second book?

Today's Scripture Passage
Acts of the Apostles, Chapter 2

The story of Pentecost is a wonderful story, and a familiar one. Let's turn our attention to the after effects. The words from verses 42 on describe the community life of the earliest followers of Christ. This sums up Christianity at its best. It should be what every follower of Christ aspires to. All the elements of Christianity are here: breaking bread and praying together, experiencing wonders and signs, sharing so no one goes without, praising God, and spreading the Good News. We know from Paul's Letter to the Corinthians, for example, that early Christian communities had their struggles. Certainly this first Christian community in Jerusalem does too. But it is clear that much excitement and energy surround this new, liberating message the Apostles are teaching. Lives are being changed and souls are being saved.

Think About . . .

What would it be like to have been taught by the very people who lived with Jesus and heard him speak?

Today's Scripture Passage

Acts of the Apostles, Chapter 3

Verses 1–10 tell the wonderful story of a crippled beggar who asks for nothing but a few coins as he does every day at the entrance to the Temple. But this day is different. Peter and John both look the beggar in the eye, which very few people ever do to beggars; in fact, most people usually make a point to look the other way. Peter even asks the beggar, whose head is probably down, to look at them. When they make eye contact, Peter delivers his message: Sorry, we have no cash to give you, but what we have is a whole lot better. Grab my hand, and in the name of Jesus Christ, get up! And so he does. The healed beggar goes crazy with joy—he jumps up and down, and everyone who sees him recognizes him, of course, and they are amazed. This miraculous public healing proves that Peter has inherited the healing power of Christ. The name of Jesus works miracles!

Think About . . .

Today try to look someone in the eyes, especially someone most people ignore.

Today's Scripture Passage
Acts of the Apostles, Chapter 4

Peter is at his spirit-filled best as he addresses the
Jewish leaders. He and John have been arrested
because all this activity is really shaking up the
leaders. They forbid John and Peter to mention the
name of Jesus. Peter has a wonderful response in
verse 20: There is simply no way we're going to
keep our mouths shut about all that we've seen
and heard. Is this the same Peter who so many
times in the Gospels fell short and even denied
knowing Christ? Yes, it is, but this is the new and
improved Peter, and there's no stopping him now;
he is on fire. Peter proves himself a fearless witness to the power of the name of Jesus. It seems
that Jesus really did pick the right man to carry on
the Good News.

Think About . . .

Just think of the energy and grace Peter felt
flowing through his veins. Pray for the courage to share with others how much your faith
means to you.

Today's Scripture Passage

Acts of the Apostles, Chapter 5

Another trial, another defiant response by Peter, another order to keep silent. This time, however, the stakes are much higher for the Apostles, because there are a few leaders who want these troublemakers put to death. But logic, not emotion, wins the day. Gamaliel, a teacher of the Law, offers a simple solution. His basic message is that this has happened before. Other so-called Messiahs have come and gone. They had lots of followers, but once the leader was killed, the followers disappeared. Most likely, the same thing will happen here. Then we'll know this is not from God. But if this movement really is from God, then there's nothing we can do to stop it; in fact, we might end up fighting God, so let's let things play out as they will. Gamaliel's logic convinces the leaders. The Apostles are whipped and told to stay quiet, but they are released. They, of course, continue to spread the Good News.

Think About . . .

Recall and reflect on a situation you've been in where logic prevailed.

Today's Scripture Passage
Acts of the Apostles, Chapter 6

The number of believers is growing. It is time for the Twelve to add some official assistants. They decide to choose seven men from among the community. Remember that the numbers 7 and 12 symbolize completeness and perfection. The Apostles ask the community to choose the seven, and they do. We are given names, but the only one that stands out is Stephen. He is described as a person filled with faith and the Holy Spirit. Suddenly the spotlight shifts from Peter to Stephen, who is working signs and wonders and proves to be an effective speaker and teacher. Once again people feel threatened, and before you know it, Stephen is arrested and brought up on charges of blasphemy, as was Jesus. False witnesses are brought forth, again just as happened with Jesus. The final verse of the chapter is telling: they all fix their eyes at Stephen and see that his face is like that of an angel.

Think About . . .

Some people just seem destined for greatness. Why do you think that is?

Today's Scripture Passage
Acts of the Apostles, Chapter 7

This chapter ends with the story of the first Christian martyr, Stephen. Unfortunately he is the first of many early Christians who die for their faith. In fact, the witness of the martyrs was very inspiring to the early Christians. It is hard not to notice that Luke deliberately draws parallels between Jesus's death and Stephen's. Both entrust their spirit to God as they are dying, and both forgive those who have inflicted death upon them. What did Stephen do or say to cause his death? He simply described his vision of the glory of God and Jesus at the right hand of God. That pretty much sealed his fate. Everyone picked up a stone and rushed him. Another "star" of the Acts of the Apostles is introduced at the end of the chapter. His name is Saul.

Think About . . .

Why is it so important for the writer of Luke and the Acts of the Apostles to show the connections between Jesus and Stephen?

Today's Scripture Passage

Acts of the Apostles, Chapter 8

The story of Philip and the Ethiopian is an interesting one. Here the Ethiopian is reading Isaiah but says he does not really understand what he is reading, and so Philip explains the passage and tells him all about Jesus. The eunuch is so moved that he wants to be baptized immediately. The chariot stops, Philip baptizes the Ethiopian, and as it ends, Philip disappears, much like the risen Christ disappeared at the breaking of the bread in the Emmaus story. What really happens is what we would call catechesis. Philip teaches the Ethiopian, who clearly wants to know more, all about the Good News. And so begins the movement of Christianity in an ever-widening circle, beyond the bounds of Judaism.

Think About . . .

The hunger for understanding marks a mature believer. Do you have that hunger?

Today's Scripture Passage
Acts of the Apostles, Chapter 9

When Ananias is told to seek out Saul and re-store his sight, Ananias hesitates, because he knows how Saul has treated the followers of Christ. God explains that Ananias has nothing to fear; Saul is the chosen one. So often God's choice doesn't seem to make sense. Abraham was an old man, too old to start a family. David was very young, the least of Jesse's sons. Peter was a rather impulsive, cowardly man who end-ed up leading the Church. And now Saul, who has been rounding up Christians and arresting them, has been chosen to be the greatest mission-ary the Church has ever had. Clearly God knows what God is doing, and God's choices turn out to be brilliant ones. That says a lot to us about whom we choose. God rarely goes with the obvi-ous or popular choice.

Think About . . .

Who are the current top celebrities? Where will they be ten years from now? Remember, the true stars in God's eyes aren't on anyone's top-ten list.

Today's Scripture Passage
Acts of the Apostles, Chapter 10

Cornelius, a good religious man, sees an angel who tells him to invite someone named Simon Peter to his home. The next day, Peter himself has a vision of all the creatures being lowered from the skies, and he hears a voice telling him to kill and eat. Why? Jewish dietary law has some very clear taboos about what can and cannot be eaten. Suddenly God is telling Peter that it's all okay. This is rather startling to Peter, an observant Jew. The two visions come together the next day when Peter is summoned to the home of Cornelius, a Gentile (non-Jew). Ordinarily Peter would not have entered a Gentile's home. But this is a new world, one with different boundaries. Peter realizes he is being called to share the Good News with this man's family and friends. And so he does. Peter realizes that this thing he is caught up in is forcing him to think bigger than he ever dreamed.

Think About . . .

Why do you think some people hold back when it comes to dreaming big?

Today's Scripture Passage

Acts of the Apostles, Chapter 11

A new word enters into the vocabulary of the time: *Christian*. Because a lot of Gentiles are being converted to following Christ, the Jerusalem community sends Barnabas to Antioch to find out what is going on there. Barnabas is impressed with what is happening in Antioch, so he goes to Tarsus and invites Saul to join him. The term *Christian* is a big step for the early Church because it begins to identify the followers of Christ as a distinct group. We can tell by the beginning of this chapter that the Jewish believers in Christ struggle with the very idea that a non-Jew could be a believer. Peter realizes this, and Paul will base his life on it, but this first step, which distinguishes Christianity as separate from Judaism, is going to cause some conflicts ahead. This new identity will take a while to settle in as reality.

Think About . . .

Why is it so important for a team or organization to have a name?

Today's Scripture Passage

Acts of the Apostles, Chapter 12

You just can't keep a good man down. Perhaps you've heard this saying. It certainly applies to Peter. Herod has him arrested and thrown into prison, with several guards watching him and double chains holding him. An angel comes to him in a dazzling light and calmly leads him out of prison. At first Peter thinks he is dreaming or having a vision. When he realizes he really is free, he rejoins the Christian community gathered in prayer, much to their astonishment. These early days of the Church are marked with so many wonders. Being freed from prison is also a meta-phorical message for the freedom Christ gives to believers. Many people are freed from all sorts of prisons, thanks to the power of prayer and faith. It is a reminder that no situation should make us despair. There is always a way out for a believer.

Think About . . .

What kind of chains are holding you back? Who has served as a "rescuing angel" in your life?

Today's Scripture Passage

Acts of the Apostles, Chapter 13

This chapter marks the first of Paul's great missionary journeys throughout the Mediterranean world.
You'll notice that he is referred to as both Saul
and Paul. This signifies his dual identity as both a
Jew and a Roman citizen. Paul and Barnabas are
sent by the Christians of Antioch to Cyprus. If your
Bible has a map, take a minute to find Cyprus,
an island off the coast of modern-day Syria. Paul
and Barnabas travel across the island, preaching in the synagogues, and they encounter a
magician, a false prophet. In these early days of
Christianity, it is very important to Paul to keep the
Christian message of salvation pure, without any
sense of magic or darkness.

Think About . . .

What is the difference between miracles and
magic? Why is this distinction so important?

Today's Scripture Passage
Acts of the Apostles, Chapter 14

Most of us are familiar with the pantheon of Greek gods: Zeus, Hermes, Apollo, Athena, Hades, Poseidon, Aphrodite, Ares, and so on. They are a colorful and fascinating bunch, and there are lots of famous stories about their powers and escapades. It is important to remember, however, that in the first century, there are still many people who believe in and worship these gods. This chapter makes that point clear when the people of Lystra, so struck by Paul's healing of a cripple, just assume that Paul and Barnabas are the gods Zeus and Hermes in disguise. It is difficult for Paul to convince them otherwise; in fact, after Paul's preaching, they are still ready to offer sacrifice to them. This is a good example of one of the many cultural challenges the early Church faced.

Think About . . .

It is often difficult to get people to see things differently, particularly in the area of religion and faith. What examples can you think of from your own life?

Today's Scripture Passage

Acts of the Apostles, Chapter 15

The ritual of circumcision performed on Jewish males was a key sign of their entrance into Judaism. The Jewish Christians of the time reason that anyone who follows Christ must observe Jewish Law, because, of course, Jesus himself was Jewish. It seems logical, but both Peter and Paul weigh in on the opposing view. Christ came for all people, not just the Jews. This is still a challenge for a lot of the Jewish Christians. It is hard for them to expand that notion. If following Christ frees people from the restrictive Jewish laws, then it doesn't make sense that non-Jews have to observe Jewish traditions before they can be baptized. Why put so many needless roadblocks before the Gentiles? Christianity is clearly coming into its own.

Think About . . .

It is sometimes hard to let go of what we are used to and see things in a new way. How have you experienced this?

Today's Scripture Passage
Acts of the Apostles, Chapter 16

Another dramatic prison rescue occurs in this chapter. This time it is Paul and his companion Silas, and it happens in Philippi in modern Greece. They have been accused of disturbing the peace and are first whipped and then imprisoned. At midnight, however, an earthquake breaks their chains and opens the doors. One of the results of this amazing event is the conversion of the jailer and his entire family. Paul pulls a trump card also: it is forbidden to beat a Roman citizen, and Paul, born in Tarsus, is a Roman citizen. The magistrates of the city are very upset that this has happened, so they release Paul and Silas and ask them to leave the city. Once again faith in Jesus Christ results in his followers' being freed from their chains, plus an entire family becomes Christian.

Think About . . .

How do the members of your family support one another in faith?

Today's Scripture Passage
Acts of the Apostles, Chapter 17

When Paul arrives in Athens, he is dismayed at seeing so many idols. He spends time talking with various philosophers, and soon he is invited to speak to the whole city. This is quite a moment for Paul. This is his opportunity to let the Athenians know about Jesus and the new revelation of God that he is so eager to share. Notice how he speaks much more of God than of Jesus. He notices an altar with the label "To an Unknown God." Paul uses philosophical and theological language to teach that the unknown god is the God that Jesus reveals. The stumbling block for many of the listeners is Paul's mention of resurrection, which makes no sense to a lot of people. He does not sway a lot of listeners, but some do become believers, including Dionysius, a member of the high Athenian court.

Think About . . .

Paul generally starts his explanations with a point that he knows his listeners already grasp. Why is it a good idea for all of us to meet people where they are?

Today's Scripture Passage
Acts of the Apostles, Chapter 18

We discover a few important things about Paul
in this chapter. First, we learn his profession. He
is a tent maker. Because many people are nomads at this time, tent making is probably a solid
profession. At times Paul probably enjoys just
working on a tent, given all of his travels and all
the things he has to endure. We also learn about
his friends Priscilla and her husband, Aquila, who
live in Corinth. Paul stays in Corinth for a year
and a half. No doubt he appreciates just staying
put after so much traveling. This explains how he
gets to know the Corinthian church so well and
becomes so concerned about it. Remember how
many issues he writes about in his letters to the
Corinthians, especially the divisions within the
community.

Think About . . .

Try to picture Paul, worn out from all his travels,
sitting in the backyard of his friends' home.
What kind of things do you think they talked
about?

Today's Scripture Passage
Acts of the Apostles, Chapter 19

In this chapter, a riot breaks out over the goddess Artemis. Ephesus had a great temple dedicated to Artemis, and it is one of the seven wonders of the ancient world. Naturally, Ephesian silversmiths make a very good living making miniature shrines to Artemis. When they get word of Paul's preaching against idols, they get very upset. Their livelihood is being threatened. They simply are not open to hearing about Jesus and the One True God that Paul and his companions talk about. They just keep shouting. Finally, someone calms them down and reassures them that these men do not mean to insult Artemis and that they could all get into trouble if they keep this up. The silversmiths simply have too much at stake. They refuse to open themselves to another reality.

Think About . . .

How often do money and profit get in the way of change and conversion? Is shouting someone down and not letting him or her speak ever the right thing to do?

Today's Scripture Passage
Acts of the Apostles, Chapter 20

There are a couple things to note here as Paul prepares to wrap up his third missionary journey and return to Jerusalem. One is that here as well as a few other times in the Acts of the Apostles, the narrator shifts from third to first person. In verse 6, the pronoun *we* occurs as it did in 16:10–17. Perhaps the writer of the Acts of the Apostles is himself one of the companions of Paul and so includes himself. It could also be a way of making the events more immediate or giving them an eyewitness quality. Also noteworthy is that Paul, in his farewell speech at Miletus, quotes Jesus: "It is more blessed to give than to receive" (verse 35, NRSV). This quotation does not occur in any of the Gospels. It reminds us that oral tradition helped form the Gospels, and that many more of Jesus's sayings are not recorded in the four Gospels of the Bible.

Think About . . .

Think of a relative who is no longer alive. What are some of the sayings she or he would repeat, or what stories have you heard about her or him?

Today's Scripture Passage

Acts of the Apostles, Chapter 21

It's hard not to admire Paul in this chapter. He is determined to go to Jerusalem. Some might even say he is stubborn. Clearly he has made up his mind, despite the pleas of several friends and believers. They really are concerned for him, but Paul will hear none of it. He is convinced he needs to go to Jerusalem and face whatever awaits him there; in fact, he says in verse 13 that he is prepared even to die there for the name of the Lord Jesus. Where does that kind of courage come from? Saints and heroes seem to possess a single mindedness that is almost frightening in its intensity. They have no doubt that what they are doing is God's will and their own destiny. And on they go.

Think About . . .

Whom do you know, or whom have you heard or read about, that has this sort of determination? Could you see yourself acting similarly about something you believe strongly in?

Today's Scripture Passage

Acts of the Apostles, Chapter 22

Paul is given an opportunity to speak to the Jews
of Jerusalem, who have already had him arrested.
He begins by doing what every skilled speaker
does: he identifies with his listeners. He is a Jew
like them. He was brought up in Jerusalem and
taught by Gamaliel, like many of them. He is a
strict observer of the Law, like them, and has even
arrested and persecuted followers of Jesus. He
stood by and watched Stephen being stoned to
death. He was on his way to Damascus to round
up a few more followers when his conversion
happened. This is the second time in the Acts of
the Apostles that we hear his story (see 9:1–9).
However, as soon as he mentions that God has
sent him to the Gentiles, the crowd loses it. They
simply cannot handle the fact that Paul is sent to
witness to non-Jews. Gentiles are not God's Chosen People, after all. This is it. He should be put
to death!

Think About . . .

Why do you think Paul's mission to the Gentiles
is such a threat?

Today's Scripture Passage
Acts of the Apostles, Chapter 23

What happens to Paul in this chapter sounds a lot like a movie plot, especially his transfer to Caesarea. He is so hated by some of the Jerusalem Jews that forty of them form a conspiracy to make sure he is killed. But Paul's nephew gets word of the plan and reports it to the commander. Paul is whisked away in the night, guarded by several soldiers who carry a letter for the governor to clue him in on what's going on. Through it all, Paul, who by now is used to surprises and twists of fate and miraculous rescues, prepares for the next episode. What's on his mind, though, are most likely the words spoken to him by the Lord: "Take courage. You're going on to Rome, and I will be traveling with you." That journey to the heart of the Roman Empire would be by far Paul's longest journey and potentially, the most dangerous. Never a dull moment for the missionary from Tarsus!

Think About . . .

Recall a situation you have been in where telling on someone was clearly the right thing to do.

Today's Scripture Passage
Acts of the Apostles, Chapter 24

Several times now, Paul has referred to the Way, as he does here in verse 14. We hear people use this word in common expressions: Can you show me the way? I've lost my way. I'm on my way. The word *way* seems more like a verb than a noun. It implies a movement, a direction, a path. To be a follower of the Way, as Paul is, is to take another road than that of traditional Judaism. Paul's adversaries refer to this as "the sect of the Nazoreans" (verse 5), because they are following Jesus of Nazareth. Paul tries time and time again to explain to the Jews that he is not trying to start a riot; he is merely telling people about the Way, the way to God through Jesus. Paul is on his way to Damascus when he is given a new Way to do God's will. His wholehearted acceptance of this new Way in his life has begun to change the world, just as his accusers claim.

Think About . . .

Do you think you are on the Way? Why or why not?

Today's Scripture Passage

Acts of the Apostles, Chapter 25

Paul must be getting weary of this chess game he is involved in. He finally appears before Porcius Festus, the new procurator, and asks to bypass Jerusalem and appeal directly to Caesar. Remember, Paul is a Roman citizen and has that right. He wants to go straight to the top and get the case against him resolved. Festus has a hard time understanding exactly what Paul is accused of. His role is not unlike that of one of his predecessors, Pontius Pilate, who also sent Jesus on to Herod at one point, because he could find no compelling reason to have Jesus executed. The person whom Paul will see next is a descendant of Herod, King Agrippa, and his sister Bernice.

Think About . . .

Have you ever felt like a pawn on a chessboard? In the game, the pawn is used by others for their own gain. In what ways is Paul like a pawn? In what ways is he not?

Today's Scripture Passage
Acts of the Apostles, Chapter 26

This chapter contains a third account of Paul's conversion, but notice the differences here. Because he is speaking to a fellow Jew, Paul emphasizes his Jewishness. He speaks of being a devout Pharisee, which implies that he is a strict observer of the Jewish religion. He speaks of the prophets and the Messiah and shows how Christ fulfills those prophecies. Paul is apparently so convincing that King Agrippa jokes with him that he is trying to convert everyone to Christianity. Interestingly Agrippa, Festus, and Bernice all agree that Paul has done nothing to merit death or imprisonment. The purpose of this episode is most likely to demonstrate that Paul is innocent and that the charges brought against him are fabricated and have no legal weight. This gives Paul a chance to appear before an impartial jury, so to speak, which finds him innocent on all charges.

Think About . . .

Have you heard a good talk lately? What made it so good and worth listening to?

Today's Scripture Passage

Acts of the Apostles, Chapter 27

What a contrast to the last few chapters! Suddenly we are caught up in a dramatic account of a sea voyage. It is easy to picture the adventure, as the details are so clearly presented. It almost seems as if we are reading the *Odyssey*, which of course every Greek and Roman knew well. It also takes Paul and his readers far out to sea, which signifies chaos and confusion. Notice again how the narrator shifts between first and third person, which has the effect of placing us in the action as well as observing it. Paul emerges as the calm hero, as he should. His prophecy about staying in Crete proves accurate. In verse 25, we have a clear Eucharistic reference as Paul takes the bread, blesses it, and breaks it.

Think About . . .

It is easy to get frightened, but we are reminded that no matter how bad the storm, we are not alone on the ship. How have you felt tossed about lately?

Today's Scripture Passage

Acts of the Apostles, Chapter 28

This final chapter of the Acts of the Apostles almost seems to be unfinished. Does Paul ever get to address the emperor? What happens next? The ending may seem flat, but really it is the logical ending of this writer's two books, sometimes referred to as Luke-Acts. Recall that throughout, the writer is trying to show how Christ came for all people. Acts of the Apostles 1:8 talks of the followers of Christ being witnesses "to the ends of the earth." In many ways, that is what Rome symbolizes for the Jewish Christians. Paul has been evicted from Jerusalem, the center of Judaism, and ends up in Rome, the capital of the mighty empire that spread from England to Africa to Asia Minor. He is under house arrest but spends two years sharing his faith and telling the Good News to all who will listen. Paul is eventually martyred in Rome, but the Acts of the Apostles is not Paul's biography. It is, from beginning to end, the inspiring story of the beginning of Christianity.

Think About . . .

What have you found most inspiring in the Acts of the Apostles?

Today's Scripture Passage
Daniel, Chapter 1

Although the Book of Daniel centers on the hero Daniel in Exile in Babylon, it was written by an unknown author some four hundred years later, around 164 BC, during the reign of Antiochus IV Epiphanes. In the first chapter, we are introduced to Daniel and his three companions whose names are changed to Shadrach, Meschach, and Abednego. They are trained in the Chaldean language and literature for eventual service to the king. As verse 17 states, these four men have the gifts of keen intelligence, and Daniel is also able to interpret visions and dreams. Faithful to Judaism throughout their training, they are a cut above the servants around them; in fact, the king finds them ten times better than all the magicians and enchanters in his kingdom. So begins the message of Daniel: Those who remain faithful to Jewish Law while serving a foreign king will thrive.

Think About . . .

Why do we all need stories of heroes? What do these stories do for us, especially in hard times?

Today's Scripture Passage
Daniel, Chapter 2

The next few chapters in the Book of Daniel each contain stories that show the superiority of God over the false gods of Babylon. In this chapter, the story centers on a dream the king has. We are reminded of the story of Joseph, whose ability to interpret dreams earned him great favor in Pharaoh's court (see Genesis, chapter 41). Here the king seems to make an outrageous demand—not just that his disturbing dream be interpreted, but that his wise men actually tell him what the dream was. Because no one seems able to pull this off, the king orders all wise men put to death. When Daniel finds this out, he asks his companions to pray for mercy. Lo and behold, Daniel can tell the king both what he dreamed and what it means. The king is impressed, and Daniel gets a big promotion. God scores again!

Think About . . .

This vision of the rise and fall of kingdoms is meant to give hope to an oppressed people. How so?

Today's Scripture Passage
Daniel, Chapter 3

Shadrach, Meschach, and Abednego refuse to worship the idol that King Nebuchadnezzar has set up. The king is furious with them, especially because they are administrators of Babylon. When the king threatens to hurl them into the furnace, the three calmly reply that there is no need for them to defend themselves (see verses 16–18). If God saves their lives, wonderful! If God does not save them, no problem. Note that it really doesn't matter to the three men what the outcome is. They know who they are, and they will not waver. This is the kind of faith that inspires us as well as the readers of the time, who are suffering their own hard times. God delivers, but even if God doesn't, our faith must not waver. What a gift, to have such strong faith!

Think About . . .

Many of us seem to have a conditional faith. We make bargains with God and base our faith on the outcome. What's the problem with that approach to God?

Today's Scripture Passage
Daniel, Chapter 4

The bigger they are, the harder they fall. Here that familiar saying applies to the mighty King Nebuchadnezzar. This story is told in first person by the king himself, almost as a proclamation. What is this really about? Humility. The constant danger of having power and wealth is the chance of forgetting who we really are. Daniel warns the king about the meaning of his dream, and sure enough, a year later it happens just as Daniel foretold. The king is humbled and then restored to his former position. It is a story of conversion. Did this really happen to Nebuchadnezzar? Maybe, maybe not. But that's not the point. It is a lesson in humility, a reminder to all rulers of who is really in charge. It is easy to forget sometimes, especially when you're at the "top of the world."

Think About . . .

Why is it hard for some people to stay humble when they've become famous? What can a person do to stay humble?

Today's Scripture Passage
Daniel, Chapter 5

This is another story with a familiar plot: a mysterious thing happens, the king calls in all his wise men to decipher what it means, and they can't do it. You have to wonder why they are considered so wise! Here the concern is quite literally the handwriting on the wall. Daniel is called in to read the words and interpret their meaning. Scholars tell us that they all have to do with weights and measures, but also that as Daniel interprets them, he plays on the meaning and sound of the words. This points us to one of the biggest problems with translating the Bible into another language. Inevitably you lose the elements of wordplay, which most times simply cannot be translated. Because over two thousand years separate us from the author who wrote this book, no doubt much of the richness of these Aramaic words and their resemblance to other words is lost.

Think About . . .

What three words do you think God would write on your wall? Why?

Today's Scripture Passage
Daniel, Chapter 6

This chapter contains the story of the lions' den, which most people associate with Daniel. Why was Daniel sentenced to such a horrible death? Jealousy. Verse 4 tells us that Daniel far outshines the other supervisors, and because his record is clear, they can find no way to bring him down. There is nothing to charge him with, so they convince the king to issue a proclamation designed to trap him. The story provides a great example of what jealousy and envy can drive people to do. Of course, in this case, it backfires, and Daniel's accusers and their families end up meeting the very fate they had hoped for him. Once again Daniel serves as a model believer, whose unwavering faith is rewarded with life. Just as his companions survived the fiery furnace, Daniel survives the lions' den. God saves!

Think About . . .

In Catholic Tradition, envy is one of the seven capital sins. Reflect on when you have felt envious of someone. How did you deal with it?

Today's Scripture Passage
Daniel, Chapter 7

Now we venture into a whole new type of writing called apocalyptic. The word *apocalypse* comes from Greek and means "revelation." The key is to know that it is symbolic. That is not too hard to comprehend, as Daniel's vision involves four giant beasts' emerging from the sea. Right away we know we are in a world that is not meant to be taken literally. How are we to interpret the symbols and images, which are used as a sort of code? The Jews of the time can decipher them, but the Greeks who rule over the Jews cannot. The challenge for modern biblical scholars is to try to determine what exactly is being referred to. We don't have to understand it all to get the over-riding message: God is the ultimate victor!

Think About . . .

Think about a recent dream you had. How do you think others might interpret that dream? How did you interpret it?

Today's Scripture Passage
Daniel, Chapter 8

It is important to understand that the enemy here is Antiochus IV Epiphanes, the worst of the Seleucid kings, who usurped the throne and wants to turn the land of the Jews into another Greek province. His greatest offense is desecrating the holy places by erecting statues to the Greek gods. So the "little horn" referred to in Daniel 7:8 and 8:9 refers to Antiochus but never mentions him by name. The four kingdoms referred to are the conquerors of Judea—the Babylonians, the Medes, the Persians, and the Greeks. The angel Gabriel, who makes his first biblical appearance here, explains some of the vision to Daniel. In the final verse, Daniel admits he doesn't really understand it. Again the point is to focus on the end times when God's greatness and power will vanquish all these enemies, especially Antiochus IV Epiphanes.

Think About . . .

Think about a recent vivid dream you had. Did it all make sense? What do you think it meant?

Today's Scripture Passage
Daniel, Chapter 9

In this chapter, Gabriel refers to seventy weeks. You may recall that numbers are almost always used symbolically in the Scriptures, but especially in apocalyptic and prophetic writing. Jeremiah had prophesied that the Babylonian captivity would last seventy years (see Jeremiah 25:11); in fact, it lasted about fifty years. Daniel is being told here that the real meaning of the seventy years is seventy weeks of years, which equates to 490 years. That would extend the period of captivity to the time the Book of Daniel was being written. In other words, even though the Persians defeat Babylon and allow the Jews in exile to return to Jerusalem, their captivity continues through a succession of conquerors to the dreaded Antiochus IV Epiphanes, who is the "he" mentioned in verse 27.

Think About . . .

Colors as well as numbers have symbolic meaning. What moods or emotions do the colors blue, red, and gray signify?

Today's Scripture Passage
Daniel, Chapter 10

Verses 18–20 contain some beautiful words of reassurance to Daniel in the midst of all his confusion and fear, words that all of us could take to heart whenever we feel overwhelmed. Twice Daniel is referred to as beloved. Twice he is told not to be afraid. Such words of comfort and encouragement! Daniel responds in words similar to this: "Speak, Lord, for you have made me feel so much better." The calming presence of God and God's message of peace and not being afraid is so often repeated by Jesus in the Gospels. In the midst of all the turbulence of life is that gentle, insistent assurance that everything will be okay. We need to take a deep breath and let God's strength flow thorough us. Good words for hard days.

Think About . . .

Repeat verses 18–20 several times slowly. Hear them as God's speaking to you. Let yourself be called beloved.

Today's Scripture Passage
Daniel, Chapter 11

The last half of chapter 11 details the history of the dreaded Antiochus IV Epiphanes. Verse 36 sums up best what this ruler is all about: he will do whatever he pleases. This sounds very much like a belief that was prominent in seventeenth- and eighteenth-century Europe. The Divine Right of Kings is the belief that the king need not answer to anyone one but God. This can be a dangerous idea, as it implies that every king acts with the sanction of God. We know from history that this is not true. When a king does what he pleases and has to answer to no one, great injustices inevitably occur. That is why prophets are so revered by the people; one of their jobs is to challenge the behavior and actions of the king. No one has the right to do what he or she pleases without being held accountable.

Think About . . .

It sounds like a great thing to be able to do whatever one pleases. However, combined with unchecked power, it can be a dangerous thing. Think about a few examples from history.

Today's Scripture Passage
Daniel, Chapter 12

The first three verses in this chapter contain a huge step forward in understanding what happens after death. Here the first clear articulation of the resurrection of the dead is proclaimed. The Jewish people always believed that those who died would live on in their children, but the idea that one who has died could come back to life is dramatic and challenging. This idea is further developed in the Book of Maccabees, which describes events that happen during the reign of Antiochus IV Epiphanes. We are so accustomed to talking about life after death that it might seem shocking that this was not always held as a common belief. It gives great hope to those who are suffering and need something to hold onto. It is not just that we live on in our children; that's good and important, but there's so much more.

Think About . . .

What does it mean to have a soul? Why is this belief so important to Christians?

Today's Scripture Passage
Daniel, Chapter 13

Depending on the Bible edition you are using, the last two chapters of Daniel may appear in a different section of the Bible. Roman Catholics consider these books inspired, just as the rest of the books of the Bible, but Protestants and Jews do not. Protestants and Jews refer to them as deuterocanonical or apocryphal books. In the story of Susanna, Daniel appears as a wise young man. This courtroom drama centers on the message Susanna utters in verse 23: It is better to stay faithful to God, no matter what the consequences. Susanna's fidelity pays off in the dramatic finish. By the way, the mastic tree is very small and the oak very large, which only serves to emphasize the lie the wicked elders tell. Daniel is the hero yet again.

Think About . . .

Here again is proof of the importance of speaking out in defense of the truth. What might keep people from speaking out?

Today's Scripture Passage
Daniel, Chapter 14

These final two stories in Daniel are entertaining, but their real purpose is to poke fun at idolatry. In the story of the dragon, Daniel once again ends up in the lions' den, but this story has different details. This tells us that Daniel's spending time in the lions' den was probably part of oral tradition. Because of that, different versions of the story developed, even though the ending is similar. Daniel, our hero throughout this book, is shown here as clearly superior to the Babylonian priests in his wisdom and in his dragon-fighting abilities. He steadfastly refuses to worship anyone but the One True God. Daniel is one consistent hero!

Think About . . .

These stories are similar to good children's stories that have a moral and teach a lesson. How would you explain the morals and the lessons for these stories?

Today's Scripture Passage
Genesis, Chapter 1

One idea in this familiar story of Creation that is
repeated each day is that God sees how good
it is. Verse 31 tells us that when God looks at everything that has been created, God finds it *very*
good. This is such an important reminder for two
reasons. First, it reminds each of us of how good
we are, created in God's image. Second, as we
become more and more aware of all the damage
we are doing to the earth, we are reminded that
our entire planet comes from the mind and hand
of God, which makes it both good and holy.
We do not have the right to treat the earth or ourselves badly or carelessly. All creation deserves
our attention, especially because we human beings have now developed the capacity to actually
destroy the earth and one another.

Think About . . .

What little steps can each of us take every day
to help heal and preserve the earth?

Today's Scripture Passage
Genesis, Chapter 2

In this second Creation story, the emphasis is a little different. The setting of this story is a lush garden we often refer to as Paradise. Here God breathes life into the first human, who is created from the clay of the earth. The first human is given the honor of naming each of the creatures. Then, so as not to be alone, God gives the human a mate, who comes from his rib, and the two become man and woman. This story clearly focuses on how closely we are tied to the earth and to one another. Verse 15 reminds us of our charge to care for the earth. It echoes the goodness of the first story and portrays God as walking on the earth, creating everything. In the end, both versions reflect the same truth: we, as well as everything around us, are created by the hand of God and given responsibility for the earth and for one another.

Think About . . .

Why do you think there are two Creation stories in the Bible?

Today's Scripture Passage
Genesis, Chapter 3

The tone of the first two chapters changes abruptly here as sin enters the world. We know the earth is good and beautiful, but we also know that a lot of evil and suffering exist in the world. How did all this happen? The author of this story tries to explain that many of the hardships in life have to do with our human weakness. We too easily give into temptation and then want to blame others for what we have done. Yes, Adam and Eve lose their innocence in this story, but they also become truly human with the free will to choose good or evil. The first two humans leave the perfect garden and enter a much more challenging world, the world we all live in. Though God may appear upset, remember that God does fashion leather clothes for the couple to wear. This is a simple gesture of kindness and protection as Adam and Eve enter a difficult world.

Think About . . .

We call the first two people Adam and Eve. How are we like them?

Today's Scripture Passage
Genesis, Chapter 4

With this chapter, violence enters our world in the form of murder. We are so accustomed to violence. It saturates our news media, entertainment, and even sporting events. Let's focus on verse 9: God asks Cain what happened to his brother Abel. God of course knows the answer, but Cain responds with a haunting question: "Am I my brother's keeper?" In other words, am I responsible for my brother? Or as we might say, do I have to keep an eye on my brother? Even though God does not respond directly to Cain, we all know the answer: Yes! We are, each of us, responsible for our brothers and sisters. How can we not be? And this means more than just our family members; we are all brothers and sisters on this planet. Notice how Cain continues that very human tendency his parents began—avoiding personal responsibility for what he has done.

Think About . . .

Should we be concerned about violent video games, television shows, and movies? How does the violence affect us?

Today's Scripture Passage

Genesis, Chapter 5

The Bible is filled with lists of generations. Why? For ancient people, much more so than for us, it was important to be able to trace family ancestry back many generations. Recall that our ancestors in the faith at first did not believe in life after death in the sense that we do. They believed that they lived on through their children and descendants. So every time someone's name is mentioned in a genealogy, that person is living on. What is striking in this chapter is how long people live. This is another example of using numbers symbolically. One interpretation is that long life is a reward from God for being a good person, so the longer people lived, the better they were. In the Bible, ages and numbers are generally not meant to be taken literally.

Think About . . .

How far back can you name your ancestors? If your family has a genealogy, check it out and thank God for each generation.

Today's Scripture Passage
Genesis, Chapter 6

After several generations, wickedness and evil seem to have flooded the earth. God, who appears very human in these early chapters of the Bible, regrets creating people, because they have used their free will to make bad choices. Washing the earth clean and starting over seems the best choice. The only good human beings left are Noah and his family. There is a lot of evidence of a great flood that devastated the Middle East in prehistoric times, because a similar story occurs in the creation stories of so many cultures. The biblical tradition is for this natural disaster to have a theological meaning. God does want creation to continue, but with a fresh start. So begins the familiar story of Noah and his ark. God establishes a covenant with Noah and his family.

Think About . . .

In this story, God seems to model the need to start over at times, to take a fresh approach, to salvage what is good and move on. How does this apply to your own life?

Today's Scripture Passage
Genesis, Chapter 7

Forty days and forty nights. Can you imagine that kind of rain? A steady downpour for almost six weeks straight. The number 40 appears often in the Bible. What is the significance of the number 40? Scripture scholars believe it is another way of saying "a long time." We think of 40 as a set number that means exactly what it is: 4 x 10, 5 x 8, and so on. However, when the Hebrew people hear the number 40 used, they automatically know the speaker or writer is saying "a long time." Obviously, for the floodwaters to cover the earth, as the story of Noah claims, it would indeed have had to rain for a long time. How long is Jesus in the desert fasting and praying? A long time. How long do the Hebrew people wander through the desert? A long time.

Think About . . .

Picture a heavy rainfall and reflect on when it changes from being a positive thing to being a negative thing. How is that like other things in life?

Today's Scripture Passage
Genesis, Chapter 8

The final verse of this chapter contains a simple but reassuring message, especially after all the chaos of the flood. Basically God is promising that as long as the earth lasts, all the familiar cycles we know will continue. Notice the order they are in: seedtime and harvest. This refers to food, of course. Cold and heat, a reality we all deal with. Summer and winter, the wonderful cycle of the seasons. And the most basic of all, day and night. Think about how we take these cycles for granted. Imagine if one day the sun just kept shining and night never came. Imagine the chaos that would cause in our lives and in the world. Thanks to science, we have knowledge of how the solar system and the universe work. But that doesn't lessen the mystery and beauty of it all. The earth keeps rotating and revolving around the sun. It is so good to be able to count on some things in life.

Think About . . .

Pause to thank God for all the natural cycles in our lives.

Today's Scripture Passage
Genesis, Chapter 9

In chapter 9, God expresses the terms of this first covenant with humankind. God promises to never again destroy the world through a flood. The sign of that covenant is the rainbow, which is a lovely, fleeting thing. We see it most often when the sun reappears after a rainfall. A rainbow can stretch across the landscape and be breathtakingly beautiful. Because it signals the end of a rainfall, it is a most appropriate sign of the covenant God articulates in this chapter: Never again will humans be wiped out through a flood. Science has explained for us how and why a rainbow exists. For ancient people, however, phenomena such as rainbows led them to connect such wonders with God. Rightfully so, as God is the author of Creation.

Think About . . .

Picture a rainbow. Let it be the focus of your meditation. Why is it such a rich symbol of God's care for us?

Today's Scripture Passage
Genesis, Chapter 10

This is the second genealogy in the Book of Genesis, and it represents an early attempt to classify the people of the world. For the writers of the first five books of the Bible, *the world* means that part of the earth that they have access to, which is Africa and Eurasia. Verse 31 mentions clans, languages, land, and nations, and this is how we categorize people yet today. A combination of geography, language, and ethnic background makes up the world as we know it. The three sons of Noah also represent three different language families and three different geographic areas of the Mediterranean world. This chapter shows both the human tendency to separate into identifiable groups as well as the important message that all of us are human beings descended from a common ancestor.

Think About . . .

In God's eyes, there is only one race—the human race. Reflect on all that binds us together as human beings.

Today's Scripture Passage
Genesis, Chapter 11

Why are there so many languages in the world? Wouldn't it be so much easier if we all spoke the same language? The story of the Tower of Babel is an effort to explain the mystery of languages. It also criticizes the human tendency to try to exist without God. For the ancient Hebrew people, Babylon symbolizes all that is wrong with humankind, and the city is famous for its towers or ziggurats. This story blames the Babylonians for their pride and also shows why so many languages exist. We have a word in English that stems from this story: *babble.* It means to talk on and on without saying anything. It certainly is not a compliment, unless it is used to describe a brook. The people stop building the tower because they can no longer understand one another. It all sounds like babble. Unfortunately language still serves as a barrier to communication today.

Think About . . .

How would our world be different if everyone spoke the same language?

Today's Scripture Passage
Genesis, Chapter 12

With the story of Abraham and Sarah, we move from prehistory into the age of the patriarchs. Abram (his original name) is the first to hear the call of God and respond. His is a remarkable story on several levels. Abram is seventy-five years old, not an age when most people could begin a new life in a foreign land. He is asked to go to Canaan with his wife and nephew and all their possessions and servants. So much is left unsaid in this dramatic story. Because Abraham is the father of our faith, the first to respond to the call of God, he is portrayed in Genesis as a man of great faith who does not hesitate to follow God's will. Abraham's courage and trust in God are traits all of us should emulate.

Think About . . .

Three major world religions trace their ancestry to Abram: Judaism, Christianity, and Islam. How could focusing on our shared heritage make the world a better place?

Today's Scripture Passage
Genesis, Chapter 13

Verse 2 reveals an interesting detail about Abram: he is very rich. We may not always picture him that way. At this time, wealth is measured in livestock, silver, and gold. In our world, property is often a sign of wealth. But it is important to remember that Abram and most people of the time are nomads, dwelling in tents and not necessarily staying in one place. This makes Abram's move to Canaan a little more understandable. As the story goes, Abram's nephew Lot also has plenty of livestock, plus the herders that take care of the animals. Abram suggests that the two of them split, so as not to create any more friction. Abram ends up in the Land of Canaan, which today is part of the state of Israel. This happened almost four thousand years ago.

Think About . . .

The only truly nomadic people in the western world are the Roma, often called Gypsies. What have you heard or what do you know about these people? What do most people think of them? Why?

Today's Scripture Passage
Genesis, Chapter 14

Verse 20 tells us that Abram gives the priest Melchizedek a tenth of everything he owns. This practice is known today as tithing. Verse 20 is the first mention of this practice in the Bible. For Abram this means one tenth of his livestock, his silver, and his gold. The purpose is to provide the priests and leaders of worship the ability to live. Today people are asked to tithe to help support the church or worshiping community they belong to. Some people do tithe. Ten percent is a substantial amount. At times this is referred to as sacrificial giving, especially if it hurts a little. That's the point. When we think of how easily and readily we spend money on all kinds of things, why is it so hard to set aside ten percent for God?

Think About . . .

If you practiced tithing right now, how much would you be giving to your church? How much *do* you give?

Today's Scripture Passage
Genesis, Chapter 15

The word *covenant* is an important word in the
Bible, occurring over and over. We encountered
it in the story of Noah, and now God makes an
important covenant with Abram, promising him
countless descendants and land. The promise of
countless descendants is puzzling to Abram because he and his wife are childless and are already senior citizens! "The Promised Land" raises
some concerns for Abram as well, because other
people already live on those lands. This covenant
between Abram and God is repeated several
times in the following chapters. Even though
Abram must have some doubts about how he will
become the father of many nations and possess
the land, he chooses to believe in God and the
promise of the covenant that he and God make
with each other.

Think About . . .

Abraham, as Abram is later called, is often referred to as a model of faith. How does he live
up to that reputation here?

Today's Scripture Passage
Genesis, Chapter 16

Customs at the time of Abram are very different from our own. It may seem bizarre that a married woman would give her husband permission to have sexual intercourse with one of her maids, but what is key here is that Abram has descendants. Because Sarai is not able to get pregnant, she consents to have her maid take her place, so to speak. We know that the story does not play out well, and to escape a difficult situation, Hagar, the maid, runs away into the wilderness. However, she is protected by God and is asked to return to the home of Sarai and Abram. She does bear a son named Ishmael. God makes a promise to Hagar that is similar to the one God made with Abram, but as we shall find out soon, it is not through Ishmael that the covenant with Abram will be fulfilled.

Think About . . .

Jealousy plays a role in this story. What does jealousy often do to people?

Today's Scripture Passage
Genesis, Chapter 17

In this chapter, a few important things take place. Abram and Sarai both experience a slight name change, becoming Abraham and Sarah, the names we know them by. The covenant is renewed with Abraham, but now at age 99, he is asked for a sign of his commitment to this covenant. That sign is circumcision. From that time on, all male descendants of Abraham and followers of God must be circumcised eight days after birth. Jesus himself was circumcised (see Luke 2:21). Today circumcision is practiced among observant Jews and Muslims, and the ritual Jewish ceremony is referred to as a *bris*. In the United States, circumcision is commonly practiced on infant males for medical or hygienic reasons. Because circumcision is permanent, it serves as an apt symbol of God's permanent covenant with Abraham and his descendants.

Think About . . .

What covenant relationships are you aware of?

Today's Scripture Passage
Genesis, Chapter 18

So who are these mysterious men who visit Abraham and Sarah and make Sarah laugh? As the story unfolds, it is clear that God is visiting along with two angels (see 19:1). In the early books of the Bible, God, in several instances, takes on human form to walk the earth. The key to such an event is hospitality. In biblical cultures, it is very important to make visitors feel welcome and at home. Notice how gracious Abraham is to these strangers. He bows to them, has water brought so their dusty feet can be washed, and tells Sarah to prepare a meal for them. In turn, the guests make an amazing promise: in a year, Sarah will give birth to a son! How can she help but laugh at such an impossible thing? Ah, but as we see many times in the Bible, nothing is impossible with God.

Think About . . .

We are taught as children not to trust strangers. How do you balance this lesson with being hospitable?

Today's Scripture Passage
Genesis, Chapter 19

Lot's wife turns into a pillar of salt in verse 19. What is the message here? God commands Lot to flee the wicked city of Sodom. Lot takes with him his wife and daughters, and they go to a safe place. Who knows why Lot's wife looks back? Perhaps she is curious to see what is happening. But by turning around, she is not following the command of the Lord to go forward. Her looking back signals a hesitation, perhaps a second thought, maybe even a desire to go back or to live in the past. All these reasons add up to a lack of total faith, which is what so much of these early stories of our ancestors in faith are all about. It's as if the writer is saying: "Don't look back. Just keep going. Your destiny lies ahead of you, not behind you." Makes sense, right? Keep the faith and keep moving on.

Think About . . .

What happens when you hesitate or second-guess yourself? What opportunities have you missed by doing that?

Today's Scripture Passage
Genesis, Chapter 20

So what's the deal with this rather strange story of Abraham's lying about Sarah? Why would Abraham lie about Sarah being his sister instead of his wife? Simple. He is afraid. He says so in verse 19. We aren't quite sure what he is afraid of, but because of Abraham's lie, Abimelech takes Sarah for himself. But before Abimelech gets involved with her, God intervenes and tells him the truth. We have to wonder how Sarah feels about all this. She is probably afraid as well. Keep in mind that women of the time are the property of their husbands and have few, if any, rights of their own. Abraham's behavior is certainly not very noble or virtuous, and it is almost surprising that this story is included twice in the Book of Genesis. But it is also reassuring to be reminded that Abraham is human and makes mistakes as well.

Think About . . .

When has fear held you back? When has being afraid made you do something you later regretted?

Today's Scripture Passage
Genesis, Chapter 21

Finally, the promised son is born to Sarah and Abraham. As if to emphasize the miraculous nature of the birth, Abraham's age of one hundred is mentioned, hardly childbearing age! The child is given the name Isaac, which in Hebrew is Yishaq, meaning laughter. That is because of Sarah's reaction to the news that she would become pregnant. It is a wonderful name and serves to highlight the significance of names in the Bible, where almost every name is given for a purpose. For many cultures, that remains a custom. Parents choose names deliberately in our culture, but generally it is not because of the meaning of the name. Think of the names of your friends and classmates. Chances are they were given names their parents liked. For Abraham, Isaac, and Ishmael, their names have a specific meaning that reveals something about them.

Think About . . .

The ending –el in Hebrew always means "God." What biblical names can you think of with that ending?

Today's Scripture Passage
Genesis, Chapter 22

This dramatic story of Abraham and Isaac is one of the most famous stories in the Bible. Many paintings have been created depicting the scene. On a literal level, it seems hard to believe that a loving God would make such a request of any human being—especially Abraham, who has waited so long for this child. We can only imagine the anguish in Abraham's heart as he and his boy climb Mount Moriah and only Abraham knows the dreadful reason. However, what we must understand about this story is that it is about Abraham's unwavering faith. Despite how absurd the request seems, Abraham never hesitates to do what God asks. In fact, it is hard to imagine a more difficult request. Abraham passes with flying colors. The story is told to show us that Abraham truly is a model of faith and trust.

Think About . . .

How has your faith been tested? Why do some people lose faith and stop believing in God?

Today's Scripture Passage
Genesis, Chapter 23

Though this chapter seems to be about giving Sarah a proper burial, it actually centers on a real estate transaction. The Hittites are more than ready to give Abraham a proper resting place for Sarah, but Abraham insists on purchasing an entire field that contains a cave, the usual burial site for the dead. Why is Abraham so intent on buying land? Up to this point, he is what is referred to as a landed immigrant. Under the law of the time, he cannot own any land. Yet Abraham knows God promised this land to him and his descendants, so it is important that he owns at least a parcel of land to begin with. Through a typical real estate transaction of the time, and through much politeness, Abraham and Ephron, the landowner, agree on a price of 400 shekels. Biblical experts say this is a very high price, which tells us two things: (1) it is very important to Abraham, and (2) he is a wealthy man.

Think About . . .

Why is owning land so important to people?

Today's Scripture Passage
Genesis, Chapter 24

This is a lovely little story about how Isaac meets his wife, Rebekah. Abraham insists that his son marry a woman from "back home," so the chief servant is sent to find a suitable wife for Isaac. The servant prays for a sign from God about who the woman will be, and no sooner does he finish his prayer, then along comes Rebekah. The servant has received the sign he asked for, so he explains it to both Rebekah and her family. After all this, Rebekah is asked to leave her homeland to marry someone she has never met. She agrees. Once again this is a story of faith. The servant trusts that his prayer will be answered, and when Rebekah's brother Laban hears the story, he trusts the truth of it as well. Finally, and most importantly, like her relative Abraham, Rebekah is willing to start a new life in a strange land.

Think About . . .

Does God ever give us signs about what we should do?

Today's Scripture Passage
Genesis, Chapter 25

So what's the big deal about Esau's birthright, and why does Jacob make sure he gets it? The birthright is the inheritance the oldest son in the family receives from his father. Because he is the firstborn, Esau is automatically entitled to twice the amount of his brother. That is his birthright, and in this case, even though Esau and Jacob are twins, Esau was born first. A telling detail is that Jacob comes out of Rebekah's womb holding on to Esau's heel. The two boys could not be more different, and Isaac, the boys' father, favors Esau, the hairy hunter. Jacob knows this and is determined to find a way to come out ahead. Esau obviously does not comprehend how important his birthright is to his future. He is concerned only with the present and his hunger. Jacob, however, is very focused on his future, and he seizes the opportunity to get what he wants.

Think About . . .

When has someone taken advantage of you?

Today's Scripture Passage
Genesis, Chapter 26

Once again we encounter a sister-wife story that has already appeared twice in Genesis, but this time it involves Isaac and Rebekah. It is hard to believe that the same thing would happen twice to Abimelech. Scripture scholars have identified four distinct writing styles in the first five books of the Bible, and here we have an example of two of them. Recall that stories were first passed on by word of mouth, or oral tradition. Eventually they were written down. In this case, there are two versions of the story and two different writers. We don't know the names of the writers, but they are called the Yahwist and the Elohist because of the names they use for God in their writing. This helps explain some of the inconsistencies in the Bible and tells us that this is not strictly a factual history, but rather a story of events through the eyes of faith.

Think About . . .

Why are there four Gospels instead of just one?

Today's Scripture Passage
Genesis, Chapter 27

In biblical times, the second inheritance the firstborn receives from his father is a solemn blessing,
usually given shortly before the father dies. In this
chapter, Jacob also manages to get that, thanks
to his mother's help. Clearly Rebekah wants Jacob
to get it all, so she also connives to make sure
he gets the final blessing. One detail that may
seem strange to us is why Isaac doesn't simply
take back the blessing and then pray it over Esau.
It is important to understand that biblical culture
is an oral culture and that a word once spoken
is believed to have power and cannot be taken
back. A father can say the special blessing for
his firstborn son only once. That is it. No taking it
back, no repeating it. Isaac is tricked into giving
the blessing to Jacob, and Esau loses out again.

Think About . . .

Do spoken words have power? Think of a few
examples.

Today's Scripture Passage
Genesis, Chapter 28

You may have heard the phrases "Jacob's ladder" or "stairway to heaven." This is where they come from. Jacob has a dream about angels' going up and down the stairs to heaven. God is there beside Jacob, giving him the same promise God gave to Abraham. It may strike us strange that God would do this, knowing how deceptive Jacob has been; however, the message seems to be that God works through us, despite our flaws and sins. What Jacob did was wrong, yet he receives the blessing, so he is the one through whom the covenant will continue. Jacob has a wonderful response to his dream in verse 16: "Surely the LORD is in this place—and I did not know it." Jacob recognizes that the place he is in is holy and creates a small shrine to mark the spot. The word *bethel* means "house or dwelling of God."

Think About . . .

Where you can sense the presence of God?

Today's Scripture Passage
Genesis, Chapter 29

Sooner or later, it all catches up to us. That seems to be the message in this chapter. Jacob falls in love with Rachel, and his uncle Laban tells him that he must work seven years to win her hand in marriage. He does, but on the wedding night, Rachel's older sister Leah, most likely covered in veils, is the one Jacob marries, unknowingly. He is deceived by his own uncle! Jacob really can't protest too much, as he has gotten away with deceiving his own father. He has to work seven more years to take Rachel as his wife as well, so he spends a total of fourteen years in Laban's service. But because these are his own people, and because Esau is very upset with him, this seems like a good plan.

Think About . . .

How do lies and deception come back to haunt us? Is it ever okay to deceive someone?

Today's Scripture Passage
Genesis, Chapter 30

What is going on? First of all, like Sarah, Rachel cannot bear children, so she consents to have Jacob bear "her" children through one and then a second of her maidservants. Her sister, Leah, also married to Jacob, has several children with him as well. Finally, Rachel has a son she names Joseph. Notice that each of the children's names has a specific meaning, as discussed earlier. Also note that in this third generation of the covenant promise, the number of descendants is growing rapidly. It doesn't take long before the promise made to Abraham becomes real, as each of these children marries and has offspring. Slowly, steadily, a nation is emerging from the line of Abraham and Sarah. Jacob eventually becomes the father of twelve sons.

Think About . . .

Look over the names of Jacob's children. Which names are still used today in our culture?

Today's Scripture Passage
Genesis, Chapter 31

Sad to say, but this chapter paints a poor picture of Jacob. So much of his life is built on deception and now, once again, after tricking Laban, he flees with his wives and possessions and even steals some of Laban's valuable idols. There are plenty of hard feelings on both sides. Unfortunately this happens a lot in families, especially big ones. Someone is hurt by someone else. Someone says something offensive and causes a rupture. People stop talking. This can go on for years. Jacob has not only alienated his uncle Laban through his actions, but he is also returning to Canaan and will have to face Esau, the brother he deceived. In so many ways, Jacob is not much of a role model. The chapter does end with reconciliation, which is definitely a good thing all around.

Think About . . .

Are there people in your family or among your relatives who don't get along? Pray for reconciliation and healing.

Today's Scripture Passage
Genesis, Chapter 32

The last section of this chapter tells of a mysterious struggle between Jacob and a man. Jacob is by himself, and soon he finds himself wrestling all night long with an angel. At dawn they stop and Jacob is given a new and very significant name: Israel, which means "wrestled with God." This also becomes the name of the nation that is forming from the descendants of Abraham. The mysterious figure tells Jacob that he has contended with human and divine beings and prevailed, which is to say that he is truly blessed. Perhaps what this rather strange story is about is Jacob's maturity. All of us must at some point "wrestle with God," so to speak. We need to struggle with our belief, and when we have worked through that struggle, we are more mature in our faith. We have a new identity, so to speak. Jacob even receives an injury, which is a reminder to him of this monumental struggle.

Think About . . .

How have you "wrestled with God"?

Today's Scripture Passage
Genesis, Chapter 33

No one is probably more surprised than Jacob at what happens when he finally encounters his estranged brother, Esau. He has been dreading the meeting and sends ahead lots of gifts to pave the way. Jacob even bows to the ground seven times as he approaches Esau. But Esau gives his brother a big hug and cries while he kisses him. Jacob must feel overwhelmed at such a generous display of affection, especially after all he has done to Esau. All is forgiven! What a marvelous scene of forgiveness and reconciliation. Jacob introduces all his children and their mothers. It seems that time does heal wounds, and Esau is clearly delighted to be reunited with his twin brother. And so Israel returns to the Promised Land he left in haste so long ago. The covenant can now be fulfilled.

Think About . . .

How have you experienced being forgiven by someone you have hurt? When have you forgiven someone who has hurt you?

Today's Scripture Passage
Genesis, Chapter 34

What happened to Dinah is horrible, and She-chem needs to be held accountable. However, what happens in this chapter is a good example of how revenge can get way out of hand. Jacob's sons decide to take matters into their own hands to avenge their sister's rape. They pretend to strike a deal with Shechem, all the while knowing what they intend to do. They end up massacring every male, including Shechem and his father. They attack the city and carry off everything they can, including all the riches, women, and children. Jacob is horrified at what they do. There is no excusing Shechem's crime, but only he should have been punished for it. That would have been justice. This, however, is bloodthirsty revenge and violence completely out of proportion to the crime committed. This is why so many laws appear in the Book of Leviticus—to prevent this kind of vengeful violence from happening.

Think About . . .

Reflect on the difference between justice and revenge.

Today's Scripture Passage
Genesis, Chapter 35

This chapter serves as a summary of Jacob's family. With the birth of his twelfth son, Benjamin, Jacob's beloved Rachel dies. Benjamin's grandfather, Isaac, lives to the ripe old age of 180, which we understand is a symbolic number that denotes his importance and goodness. It must be gratifying for Isaac to see so many descendants around him. In the third generation, the amazing promise made to Abraham about countless descendants is well on its way to happening. Isaac also must feel great comfort in knowing that his twin sons, enemies for so long, now get along and are at his side at the end. The names of the twelve sons of Jacob become important because from each of them comes many offspring who then identify themselves as belonging to the tribes of Reuben, Simeon, Dan, and so on. Eventually each tribe settles in a defined area of the Promised Land and become the Twelve Tribes of Israel.

Think About . . .

Whom do you know that has lived a full life?

Today's Scripture Passage
Genesis, Chapter 36

This is one of those chapters where it is very easy to get bogged down in the long list of names. These genealogies are typical, as we know, and usually serve to explain how all the peoples and tribes that occupied the Middle East fit together. This chapter is devoted to Esau and his descendants, who came to be known as the Edomites, traditional enemies of the Israelites. Scripture scholars are doubtful about whether the Edomites really did come from Esau. More likely, this is an attempt to show how the neighboring Edomites, with a similar language, are connected to the Israelites. Edom is located to the southeast of Judea, and because there are very few records of the Edomites, we can only speculate about them. Eventually they disappear from history without a trace, swallowed up in the wave of conquests that follow the Babylonian invasions.

Think About . . .

Who is the earliest ancestor of your family you can name? Where is he or she from?

Today's Scripture Passage
Genesis, Chapter 37

Once again jealousy rears its ugly head and almost results in fratricide (brother killing brother). The remainder of the Book of Genesis is about Joseph. It reads almost like a short novel and starts off with Joseph's brothers detesting him because of how much their father favored him, as well as because of Joseph's dreams, which always show him as the center of attention. Is Joseph spoiled? That's pretty obvious in the fact that Jacob gives him a special robe to wear and that he does not have to tend sheep with the rest of his brothers. The brothers finally decide to get rid of Joseph by selling him to some traders on their way to Egypt. Once again Jacob is the victim of deception as his sons tell him that a wild beast has killed Joseph. Problem solved. Now Joseph is out of their lives forever. Or so they think.

Think About . . .

It is not wise for parents or guardians to play favorites. What might happen to a family if this occurs?

Today's Scripture Passage
Genesis, Chapter 38

This chapter interrupts the Joseph story and gives us some interesting history on the beginnings of the tribe of Judah. The story centers around a law called Levirate Marriage, which is spelled out in Deuteronomy 25:5–10. It decrees that if a man's married brother dies without a son, that man is obligated to marry his sister-in-law, and the first son that is born shall belong to the deceased brother. Why? To ensure that a dead man's property is passed on to his son, because women cannot own property. It is also a way of protecting the dead man's widow, as she would have no means of support. When Judah's oldest son, Er, dies, and the second son, Onan, refuses to cooperate, the third son is promised to Tamar. When Judah fails to keep his promise, Tamar tricks him into doing the right thing. The key here is that from the line of Perez will eventually come King David.

Think About . . .

How do your family members care for one another?

Today's Scripture Passage
Genesis, Chapter 39

It seems that Joseph has a lot going for him, even if he is a slave. Besides being good looking, he has obviously matured into someone who gets along with others and is trustworthy. He has a knack for organizing things and managing people, and all these gifts serve him well in Egypt, except his good looks. Potiphar's wife wants to seduce him, but Joseph refuses to violate his master's trust, and because of that Potiphar lies about him and he is thrown in jail. But even there, Joseph's God-given abilities and talents shine, and soon he is in charge of all the prisoners. The chief jailer trusts him completely. Despite the cruelty of his brothers and the injustice he has experienced, Joseph is determined to make the best of wherever he is. It seems that the "spoiled brat" has grown up a lot!

Think About . . .

We always need to give one another room to grow and mature. Whom can you think of that has matured and changed for the better?

Today's Scripture Passage
Genesis, Chapter 40

Here another of Joseph's talents is on display. Recall that one of the reasons his brothers detested him is that he would share his dreams. The meaning of them was painfully obvious to the brothers. Now, however, the dreamer proves himself to also be an interpreter of dreams, which is a very valuable skill to have. Notice that in verse 8, Joseph gives credit to God as the one who gives him this gift. He goes on to accurately interpret both dreams. He does ask Pharaoh's cupbearer to put in a good word for him, but the cupbearer forgets. Most of us do not take our dreams too seriously, and we probably don't even remember them very well, unless they are particularly vivid or disturbing. In biblical times, dreams had great significance. The ability to explain what a dream means could prove to be a very useful talent, as Joseph soon finds out.

Think About . . .

Recall some dreams that you have had. What connections did you make with your life at the time?

Today's Scripture Passage
Genesis, Chapter 41

From a lowly prisoner to Pharaoh's right-hand man in one day—not bad! Two years pass before Pharaoh has his dreams that no one can make sense of. All this time, Joseph is living out his unjust sentence, seemingly forgotten. Then the cupbearer remembers him, and Joseph is cleaned up and brought before Pharaoh. Joseph gives God full credit for anything that will happen. He is able to interpret the dreams, and because of his wisdom, he is given the job of overseeing the kingdom through the fourteen years of feast and famine. Perhaps you've heard the expression "Good things come to those who wait." This story is a perfect example of that. Joseph does not despair; he keeps his faith and just hangs in there. Thanks to him, Egypt is the only country prepared for the famine and is actually able to provide grain to other nations. Faith and patience serve Joseph well.

Think About . . .

How is your patience level? How good are you at waiting?

Today's Scripture Passage
Genesis, Chapter 42

This is where the story really gets good. Finally, Joseph is reunited with his brothers, but they have no idea. And why would they? They presume Joseph is a slave somewhere and would not even dare to look the governor of Egypt in the face. Joseph, who understands everything they are saying, decides to play a little trick on them. What he really wants is to see his younger brother, Benjamin. He bears his brothers no ill will, and even though he is completely justified in taking their money for the grain, he secretly gives it back to them, which only makes them more fearful. We know how hard all this is on Joseph by the comment in verse 24 that at one point he turns away from them and cries. It has been so many years since he has seen anyone from his family.

Think About . . .

Try to imagine how Joseph feels when his brothers come into his presence. What do you think is going through his mind?

Today's Scripture Passage
Genesis, Chapter 43

Now the brothers are truly confused, and we have to smile at how this is all playing out. Joseph continues to string along his brothers, but this time they are truly bewildered by the kindness and generosity he shows them. They approach Joseph's steward, expecting to be in big trouble, but instead they are told to get ready for a big meal. They do, but imagine how wary and suspicious they must be. This seems too good to be true. Joseph is overcome with joy at being reunited with his little brother, Benjamin. They are especially close because they share the same mother, Rachel. Joseph even has the brothers seated by their age and then gives Benjamin five times the amount of food and drink the others get. Finally, the brothers decide to relax and simply enjoy this most strange and unexpected party. Who knows what tomorrow will bring?

Think About . . .

So often a big meal or party is how we show affection for others. Why is this a good way to celebrate?

Today's Scripture Passage
Genesis, Chapter 44

As readers we know Joseph is behind the whole plot with the silver goblet. The brothers have no idea what is going on, but they are horrified when the goblet is found in Benjamin's bag. They all offer to be enslaved to Joseph because of this, but he says that only Benjamin needs to stay behind. Here is where Judah steps in. He tells Joseph that he pledged his life to make sure Benjamin returns home safely. Judah cannot bear what will happen if they come home without Benjamin. Jacob will never recover from the loss of both of his youngest sons. Judah's willingness to take Benjamin's place is admirable. This means he will never be able to return home and will be a slave for the rest of his life. This is how much his pledge means, and this is also how much he cares about his youngest brother.

Think About . . .

If you have brothers or sisters, do you stick up for them? How far would you go to make sure a family member is safe from harm?

Today's Scripture Passage

Genesis, Chapter 45

What a great scene! At last Joseph reveals himself to his brothers. They are dumbfounded, of course, never dreaming that Pharaoh's right-hand man is the brother they sold into slavery so many years ago. And the best part is that he bears them no ill will. In fact, he is so happy that they are reunited. Joseph also realizes now, as a man of faith, what has happened. He explains to them that yes, they did a bad thing to him, but God used that bad deed and turned it into good. Through Joseph God has been able to save lives, especially the lives of Jacob and his family. Not only that, but Pharaoh himself insists that the whole family settle in the best land of Egypt. When Jacob hears the incredible news, he knows his life will have a happy ending.

Think About . . .

So often in life good things result from something that seemed awful at first. What examples can you think of in your life or that of someone you know?

Today's Scripture Passage
Genesis, Chapter 46

Moving day for the Israelites! The whole family sets off for Egypt. We are given a roll call of each son and his offspring, which totals seventy, not counting wives and servants. It is hard to imagine a more moving reunion than that between Jacob and his long-lost son, Joseph. It really is the second such reunion in Jacob's colorful life. Many years earlier, Jacob was reunited with his twin brother, Esau, after years of separation. Jacob duped a few people in his younger life, but now as an old man, he sees his family complete again and he can die in peace. True, they are far from the land promised them, but at least they will be well taken care of during the long famine ahead. Goshen is a very nice piece of property.

Think About . . .

Moving is a reality for many families in our world today. Have you or someone you know experienced a major move to another city, state, or country? How do you see God's will in that move?

Today's Scripture Passage
Genesis, Chapter 47

The main part of this chapter is Joseph's land policy. As the famine continues and ravages the land, the Egyptians grow more and more desperate. First, they trade their livestock for grain. Then they trade their farmland for grain. Once Pharaoh has the livestock and land, the Egyptians are given seed to plant, but a fifth of the harvest belongs to Pharaoh. The people are grateful for the seed and do not realize they have slowly and steadily given Pharaoh almost everything they possess. The brilliance of Joseph's plan is that he makes Pharaoh richer while guiding the nation through the famine. When it ends, Pharaoh will have amassed incredible wealth and power, thanks to Joseph's strategy. The writer of this chapter points out that the practice of giving Pharaoh 20 percent of the harvest is still in effect centuries later.

Think About . . .

What countries are you aware of that are currently gripped by famine?

Today's Scripture Passage
Genesis, Chapter 48

Joseph has had two sons born in Egypt: Manasseh and Ephraim. Jacob adopts them as his own for a couple reasons. Because they were born in Egypt, Jacob apparently wishes to confer upon them full status as Israelites even though their mother is Egyptian. The Twelve Tribes of Israel do not include a tribe of Joseph, but rather tribes of Manasseh and Ephraim, and this incident helps explain how that happened. After Rachel's death, Jacob adopts the boys as the sons Rachel never had. Jacob then gives the two boys his blessing. He knows his days are numbered, and he is slowly getting everything together before he dies.

Think About . . .

People who know they are dying or close to death often want to get everything in order before they die. Why do you think this is an important step?

Today's Scripture Passage
Genesis, Chapter 49

The scene here is Jacob on his deathbed, surrounded by his sons. He has a word for each
of them. The son he spends the most time with
is Judah. He tells Judah that he will emerge as
the most important of the tribes, for from his line
shall eventually come the great King David. The
imagery of the lion also shows the supremacy
of the line of Judah. Eventually the Tribe of Judah
will become dominant and will give its name to
both the southern kingdom of Judea as well as to
the Israelite people themselves: the Jews. What is
most important, however, is that from Judah will
come the line of kings and eventually the Messiah. At the end of the chapter, Jacob breathes his
last. What a long and amazing life he has had.
Indeed half of the Book of Genesis is devoted to
Jacob and his sons.

Think About . . .

If you knew you were dying, what would you
say to each member of your family?

Today's Scripture Passage
Genesis, Chapter 50

It is interesting, isn't it, that after Jacob is buried, back on the piece of land purchased so long ago by Abraham, Joseph's brothers are still worried that Joseph may be out to get them for what they did to him? Joseph is clearly astounded that they would think this way and reassures them by again summing up how all of what happened is part of God's plan. Verse 20 states the theme very well. Joseph also reassures his brothers that he will continue to provide for them. No hard feelings, guys—honest! The Book of Genesis concludes with Joseph's death and burial in Egypt. He does ask that when the Israelites return to the Promised Land, they take his bones with them. And so ends the first book of the Bible, so rich with vivid stories and lively characters.

Think About . . .

Which main character in the Book of Genesis is your favorite? Why?

Today's Scripture Passage
Sirach, Chapter 1

With the Book of Sirach, we dive back into wisdom literature. The foreword is where the writer, often referred to as Ben Sira, which literally means "son of Sirach," spells out what he is up to. You'll notice many similarities between the Book of Sirach and the Book of Proverbs. The goal of both is to impart wisdom and to serve as a guideline for good moral living. One phrase that is repeated many times in this first chapter and throughout the wisdom literature is "fear of the Lord." Do not interpret this to mean being afraid of the Lord. We might use the phrase "reverence for God." *Reverence* is a rich word whose meaning falls somewhere between "respect" and "awe." For the Jewish people, it really is the definition of their faith: reverence for God, always and everywhere. One unique feature of this book is that the writer identifies himself at the end (see 50:27). His name is Jesus, son of Eleazar, son of Sirach.

Think About . . .

How do you show reverence for God in your own life?

Today's Scripture Passage
Sirach, Chapter 2

Have you ever had a dream about falling? Most of us have. Usually we wake up before we land, but it is frightening to be in a free fall. Now try to imagine falling and being caught by a giant pair of hands that gently cradle you as you land. A comforting image, right? Picture these as the hands of God. This is the image presented in the final verse of this chapter: "Let us fall into the hands of the Lord, / but not into the hands of mortals" (NRSV). This is a nice play on words. We often talk about falling into the wrong hands. That's what this is about. God's hands are big enough to catch us and hold us and keep us safe. Human hands cannot support us in the same way. Not that others aren't important to us, especially when we are in distress, but nothing can beat the security of God's hands.

Think About . . .

Close your eyes and imagine yourself in a free fall. Try to picture God's hands catching you. What does that feel like?

Today's Scripture Passage
Sirach, Chapter 3

Have you heard the expression "random acts of kindness"? It is a sort of antidote to the more common phrase "random acts of violence." By committing acts of kindness, we plant seeds that will bear fruit later. The last verse points this out by saying that those who do kind things for others will be remembered later, especially in times of need. When a kind person falls or fails, she or he will find support in others. No one will be gloating over that person's misfortune, because people know how kind she or he is. When others treat us kindly, we remember that. It reminds us to do the same, to spread kindness wherever we go. If people are going to talk about you, wouldn't you rather it be about how kind you are rather than how difficult you are to get along with? A legacy of kindness is a powerful one.

Think About . . .

Think of a random act of kindness you could do today for someone. Resolve to do it.

Today's Scripture Passage
Sirach, Chapter 4

So what do we do about someone who is begging for money as we walk by? or about the homeless person holding up a sign asking for our help? Verses 4 and 5 tell us not to turn away from those who are poor, not to look the other way from the needy person in front of us. Whether to give that person money is one issue, but to avoid even looking at that person is quite another. After all, how hard is it to at least say hello and look him or her in the eye? By doing so, you are acknowledging that person's existence and affirming his or her humanity. Too often we are scared that something might be asked of us. It's easier just to turn away. Think about it. What would it cost us to at least smile at our fellow human being who is before us in need?

Think About . . .

What is your first impulse when you encounter a homeless person or a beggar? Reflect on what you will do next time.

Today's Scripture Passage
Sirach, Chapter 5

"Be swift to hear, but slow to answer." This is how verse 13 reads in the New American Bible. It is simple and to the point and contains a true pearl of wisdom. Think about how often the opposite happens. Most of us are not very good listeners, but we are often ready to blurt out a response, especially if we are angry or annoyed. The biological fact that we have two ears and one mouth ought to tell us something. What others are saying deserves our full attention. Hearing is a sensation; we cannot help but hear sounds. Listening, on the other hand, requires our attention. "Are you even listening to me?" is something one family member might say to another. Sirach advises us to sharpen our listening skills and to be more thoughtful when we respond.

Think About . . .

Often the people we spend the most time with are the hardest ones to really listen to. Why is that? Think of one person you will strive to listen to more attentively.

Today's Scripture Passage
Sirach, Chapter 6

You would be hard-pressed to find a more poetic and accurate description of friendship than in verses 5–17. Ben Sira (the writer) provides us with a checklist of the types of friends we will meet in life. Many of them will ultimately prove to be false friends, sticking around only as long as it suits them. Others will betray our trust. The true friend, however, will slowly gain our trust over time and will prove herself of himself by standing by us, no matter what. We can usually count those kinds of friends on one hand, and that's a good thing. We need a few people that we can confide in and count on. As verses 14–16 say so beautifully, a true and faithful friend is like a strong shelter from the storms of life, is like a life-saving medicine, and is a true treasure, beyond price.

Think About . . .

Think about the people in your life who are true friends. What can you do to strengthen those relationships?

Today's Scripture Passage
Sirach, Chapter 7

There is a lot of good advice in this chapter. Let's focus on verses 34–35. As much as we would like to avoid unpleasantness in our lives, the fact is that it's all around us. If someone is sad or grieving, do we just look the other way because we are embarrassed or just don't want to deal with it? What kind of response is that? Why do we often find it hard to reach out to others in their time of need? We don't have to say much. Just let them know that we are aware of their sadness and that we care. So why not make a point of visiting someone who is ill? Make someone's day, even if it's only for a few minutes. It's not the length of time that matters; it's that you took the time.

Think About . . .

Who is someone you know that is in grief over the loss of someone or something or somebody who is sick? Think about what you can do for him or her.

Today's Scripture Passage
Sirach, Chapter 8

This chapter gives solid advice in dealing with others. Verse 16 is striking because of how practical it seems today. It warns against getting into an argument with someone who has a quick temper. Never go anywhere with this person where the two of you are alone. If this person loses her or his temper, she or he could easily resort to violence and leave you badly beaten or even dead. As children we learn not to accept anything from strangers, especially a ride. That same advice applies to any one of us! To get into a vehicle with someone we do not know puts us at immediate risk because now that person is in control of where we are headed and what will happen there. Use your common sense and trust your instincts. Avoid situations that put your safety and well-being at risk. It's just not worth it.

Think About . . .

When meeting new people or accepting invitations to go out, what steps do you take to keep yourself safe?

Today's Scripture Passage
Sirach, Chapter 9

As verse 10 mentions, it takes time to make a true friend. It doesn't happen overnight. It might be that we meet someone that we have a lot in common with and really enjoy being around. That's a good thing, but it's always a good idea to move slowly. Building a lasting friendship takes time. There will always be rough spots, but once you have a good friend, hang on to that person. Don't be quick to let that friend go. Chapter 6 gave us good advice on true friendship. We are reminded to think twice before letting go of a friend we have had for a long time and to proceed slowly with a new friend. Friendship is definitely one of life's special blessings, so we must treat as it as such.

Think About . . .

Do you have any regrets about a lost friendship? What could the two of you have done differently to save the friendship? Can you do anything now to restore it?

Today's Scripture Passage
Sirach, Chapter 10

Pride can be a confusing concept. We are told that it is essential to be proud of who we are and to take pride in what we have accomplished. So why is Ben Sira warning about the sin of pride in verses 6–18? Another word used often in those verses gives us a big clue. That word is *arrogance*. This is a telling trait of someone who has changed pride from a good thing to a negative thing. Arrogance is an exaggerated sense of oneself or one's abilities. Arrogance comes out in how people talk about themselves and others. Arrogant people seem to want you to know they are really good at something or certainly better than you are. Arrogance is the opposite of humility, which means being aware of both our weaknesses and our strengths. We are proud of the latter and working to improve the former.

Think About . . .

What examples of arrogance can you think of? How do you deal with arrogant people? Are you guilty of arrogance?

Today's Scripture Passage
Sirach, Chapter 11

In biblical times, the transmission of wisdom and knowledge was almost always oral. Listening, therefore, was essential to learning. Verse 8 offers us some helpful advice when it comes to improving our listening skills. First of all, listen to what someone has to say before you respond. And don't interrupt! By interrupting someone, you are not practicing good listening. How can you possibly be listening to someone's complete thought if you interrupt what they are saying to make your own point? Most people resent being interrupted, even if they don't say so. We want to be listened to or heard out. By not interrupting, we are showing that we are good listeners. That can make a huge difference. We may even gain a reputation as a good listener!

Think About . . .

Make a conscious effort today not to interrupt people. Make a point of being a good listener. It might be habit forming.

Today's Scripture Passage
Sirach, Chapter 12

This chapter has a lot to say about enemies. It assumes that we do have enemies, and that they are out to get us whenever they have a chance. The last two verses pretty much sum it up. This is, however, a striking contrast from what we hear in the Gospels. Jesus came delivering a very different message: love your enemies and pray for your persecutors. Can you see why this was such a radical message? Ben Sira tells us to be on guard against our enemies. Jesus of Nazareth has a very different approach, and this is what makes the New Testament new. Jesus Christ gives us a new way to regard those who are our enemies. After all, it's pretty easy to hate those who hate us. Responding to hatred with love and goodwill is really what can turn everything upside down.

Think About . . .

Do you regard anyone as an enemy, or is there someone in your life you really can't stand? If so, take a moment now to pray for that person.

Today's Scripture Passage
Sirach, Chapter 13

Once again the final two verses of this chapter contain a gem of wisdom. It's all about what's inside your heart. If evil resides there, it will show on your face. Others will notice your eyes and your expressions. If, on the other hand, your heart is filled with goodness, it will also show on your face. Most likely, your face will be a cheerful one, one that makes others feel good rather than uneasy. Though it isn't good to judge a person by first impressions, it is also true that we can learn a lot about a person by looking into his or her eyes, by observing his or her face or countenance. What do you see there? The goodhearted always seem to have a smile to give us, a way to make the lives of people around them lighter and more joyful.

Think About . . .

How do you think you come across to other people, especially when you first meet?

Today's Scripture Passage
Sirach, Chapter 14

So what do we do if we are blessed with wealth and riches? In verses 11–19, Ben Sira basically tells us to enjoy what we have and to treat ourselves, because we certainly can't take it with us. Not a bad attitude—certainly better than being stingy and miserable. But here again we realize that the Gospel message of Jesus calls us to a higher plane. Jesus speaks often of riches and poverty and clearly tells us of our obligation to give to others from what we have been given. It's not that Jesus contradicts his wise ancestor; he simply sets the bar higher and provides a much more other-centered approach to dealing with our wealth. Give to others, be generous, and in that you will be fulfilled. There is nothing wrong with treating yourself once in awhile. But it is ultimately much more fulfilling to give it away to those in need. Your generosity can literally save a life.

Think About . . .

How do you spend your money? How should you spend your money?

Today's Scripture Passage
Sirach, Chapter 15

It's up to you. Really. Don't blame someone else. Verses 11–20 couldn't be much clearer. Things haven't changed since those words were written. God gave us a precious gift: free will. We hear about it a lot, but it is so easy to misuse that gift. It seems as if we are always looking for someone else to blame when we get caught. Why is that? It started with Adam and Eve and seems to be an indelible part of the human condition. Ben Sira tells us we can't blame God when we take the wrong path or make a decision we regret. It's us. We have been shown the Way, and we choose whether to follow that Way each and every moment. It's time to grow up and to live up to our responsibilities as the free creatures we are. If we sin or stray, it's our choice. It's that simple. That's the way free will works.

Think About . . .

Think about the last time you got caught for doing something wrong. What excuses did you come up with?

Today's Scripture Passage
Sirach, Chapter 16

Four billion people live on our planet. Our galaxy is tucked away in one corner of a vast universe. Do you really think God cares about what I do or even who I am? This is the attitude presented in verses 15–20. God is much too busy to care about little ol' me and the sins I commit, right? Wrong! This is the attitude of someone with very little sense, as we are told in verse 21. God does know what we're up to, but that is not a negative. Jesus cast this thought in a positive light by telling us that every hair on our heads is numbered. Yes, God cares that much! God loves us and therefore cares about what we are doing and what is happening to us. We belong to God. That should reassure us. We are being lovingly cared for, not spied on.

Think About . . .

Try to picture God watching you with binoculars from a hilltop. Then picture God walking along beside you. Ponder the difference.

Today's Scripture Passage
Sirach, Chapter 17

"Remember, man, you are dust and to dust you will return" (*Sacramentary*, p. 77). These sobering words are sometimes heard on Ash Wednesday by those who receive ashes. Ben Sira expresses the same thought at the beginning of chapter 17. This may seem like a rather bleak attitude, but in a deeper sense, it is a stark reminder of how fleeting life really is. All of us, no matter how great or small, will eventually return to the earth. Scientists tell us our bodies are made up of the same ingredients as the universe. We are "cosmic dust," so to speak, and we become part of the earth that has sustained us. We are on this earth for only a short time, a moment in the face of eternity. Let us not waste even a moment then. So, yes, remember that you are dust, but make the most of it, knowing that eventually you will return to the earth from which God made you.

Think About . . .

How can you make the most of this day?

Today's Scripture Passage
Sirach, Chapter 18

The last four verses of this chapter are entitled "Self-Control." This term, in a way, really sums up a wise person. As the verses warn us, if you give in to all your whims and temptations, it won't be long before you will be a loser, in every sense of the word. It is advice the prodigal son in chapter 15 of the Book of Luke should have taken to heart before he headed out with all of his inheritance, only to blow it in a short amount of time. Self-control really does pay off in big dividends later on. It is habit forming, and that is a good thing in this case. You rarely hear people regret having too much self-control; rather, the opposite is generally true. We need, as Ben Sira reminds us, to keep our desires and appetites in check. Think of how many of the problems in life are caused because somebody isn't exhibiting self-control.

Think About . . .

How can you do a better job at self-control? What is one area of your life where more would really help?

Today's Scripture Passage
Sirach, Chapter 19

The eighth commandment says, "You shall not bear false witness against your neighbor" (Exodus 20:16, NRSV). If you have ever wondered what that really means, it is spelled out very well in verses 5–16. Some versions of the Bible label this section "Loose Talk." That's a good way to sum it up. It's so tempting to share something you hear about someone, especially if it is really juicy or shocking. But what's the point? Better yet, what's the justification? Some people—we all know them—just can't wait to tell you the latest about so-and-so. Why? Who knows? But to be part of that chain of gossip and rumor really is to go against the eighth commandment. You would be bearing false witness against your neighbor.

Think About . . .

What is the latest rumor going around? Have you been part of spreading it? Resolve to do better, to pull away from loose talk.

Today's Scripture Passage
Sirach, Chapter 20

"Admit when you are wrong, and you will avoid embarrassment." This is the Good News translation of verse 3. It's hard to argue with that sound advice, and yet it is not always an easy thing to do. We really don't like to admit we're wrong, especially if we have argued long and loud for our position. So many politicians seem to forget this simple truth from verse 3. They somehow feel it's a sign of weakness to admit to a mistake. What they don't realize is that it is actually a sign of strength, and generally people will react more positively to someone who can honestly admit a mistake than to someone who keeps trying to put a different spin on what she or he said to "save face." Soon a person like this gets caught in a web of words and loses respect from others. If you are wrong, admit it. Period.

Think About . . .

When have you had to admit you were wrong? Reflect on that experience.

Today's Scripture Passage
Sirach, Chapter 21

Typical of wisdom literature, verse 25 contrasts the wise person and the fool. In this case, it pertains to what we say and when we say it. A foolish person pretty much says whatever comes to mind without really thinking it through. A wise person, on the other hand, generally puts a lot more thought into what he or she says. One version of this verse says that the words of fools are in their mouths, whereas the words of wise people are in their hearts. That's a poetic way of saying that there is much more depth to what a wise person says, because what he or she says comes from a deeper place. We all know people who don't talk all that much, but when they do, we pay attention, because what they say makes a lot of sense and has a certain authority. Those who babble on generally lose the respect of their listeners because people get lost in their words, which just keep coming.

Think About . . .

Whom do you know that generally says wise things and has sound insights?

Today's Scripture Passage
Sirach, Chapter 22

Friendships are precious, but so often misunderstandings or anger can ruin them. Verse 22 advises us that even if we get into a bad argument with a friend and part ways over it, it is never too late to reconcile. Friends are gifts from God that we need to treasure. Naturally we will get upset with each other sometimes. At times we may exchange words that we later regret. That happens in almost every relationship. What we do afterwards, however, is what determines our priorities in life. If a friendship means a lot to us, we will strive to make amends, to seek out common ground, to "let bygones be bygones," as they say. The friendship will only be stronger if we work things through. That's where grace comes in. God will definitely be part of that effort.

Think About . . .

What relationships in your life need some mending? What is keeping you from taking the first step?

Today's Scripture Passage
Sirach, Chapter 23

Civility is a word you may or may not be familiar with. It means speaking respectfully and politely to others. Unfortunately in our society, civility seems to be a dying art. We have grown more and more accustomed to hearing and using foul language. It rarely shocks us anymore, and for some people, four-letter words come out whenever they talk. The problem is that as common as it may be, foul language is not appropriate in most formal settings. In fact, it can get us into trouble. Verses 12–15 address the issue of filthy talk and advise against it. The message here is that the more we use foul language, the less aware we become that we are doing so, and the more likely we are to use it at an inappropriate time. Resist the urge to curse and swear. Let civility creep back into our society!

Think About . . .

Reflect on your own use of language. How guilty are you of using foul language? Can you get through a day without using it?

Today's Scripture Passage
Sirach, Chapter 24

In this chapter, Wisdom is given a chance to speak, as in chapter 8 of the Book of Proverbs. We tend to think of wisdom as a trait, as a thing to possess, but here Wisdom is personified and is always described as feminine. It is as if Wisdom balances the often masculine imagery we are given of God. The chapter is full of beautiful passages that describe how Wisdom has been around since the beginning of time. In verses 13–19, Wisdom compares herself to a luscious variety of trees and spices. The words of verse 18 are strikingly similar to those of Jesus in Matthew 11:8, when he calls us to come to him because his yolk is easy and his burden is light. In Catholic Tradition, Wisdom is often associated with Mary, the Mother of Jesus.

Think About . . .

Try to picture Wisdom as a person, beautiful but mysterious. Which of Wisdom's passages in this chapter do you like best?

Today's Scripture Passage
Sirach, Chapter 25

Sometimes the Bible surprises us with its poetry and beauty. Some passages are so true and accurate that it seems as if they were written yesterday. At other times, however, we are startled by the negative tone of a passage and how it contrasts with what we believe to be true today. The last half of this chapter is a good example. In verses 12–25, Ben Sira goes on and on about how wicked women are, how they are to blame for all the things in the world, and how they need to be punished if they don't tow the line. Ben Sira's attitude here reflects a persistent attitude toward women that we consider sexist and offensive. It scapegoats all women and justifies harsh treatment and even abuse of women. We know in our hearts that this is not godlike behavior. And unlike most passages in this book, this one does not exemplify wise behavior.

Think About . . .

Imagine if this passage were written by a woman about men. How do you think people might react?

Today's Scripture Passage
Sirach, Chapter 26

This chapter contrasts the good wife with the bad. Passages about the good wife dominate the chapter and are complimentary to women. Many of them could be applied equally to the good husband. Keep in mind, however, that in biblical times, men are the ones who study the Bible, so they are the target audience for Ben Sira. The few passages about the drunken wife and the unruly wife again underline the prevalent attitude of the time that women are the property of their husbands, pure and simple. Notice that the "bad husband" is not referred to and that even today you don't hear the expression "a loose man" to describe a male who is sexually promiscuous. We need to read past the cultural attitudes of biblical times and strive to find the religious truth. Clearly the wise person knows that his or her spouse is a blessing and deserves to be treated with respect.

Think About . . .

Is there a double standard for men and women? Reflect on that in your own attitude toward women and men.

Today's Scripture Passage
Sirach, Chapter 27

Profit is a powerful motive. The urge to make more money is what drives our economy. The American dream is built on the idea that everyone, no matter what background, has the opportunity to make it big. Countless stories bear that out. But there are also many stories of people who have sold themselves out to achieve the American dream. Verses 1 and 2 warn us how easy it is for people to slip into sin when trying to get rich. It becomes easier and easier to cut corners, to compromise values, and especially, when high up in a big corporation, to make decisions that can negatively affect a lot of people. The gap between the haves and the have-nots seems to grow each year. There is nothing wrong with making money and being successful, but there is something wrong with cutting corners and harming others to get there.

Think About . . .

Reflect on those people who never achieve the American dream, despite their best efforts. What holds them back?

Today's Scripture Passage
Sirach, Chapter 28

In this chapter, both anger and vicious talk are compared to a flame that grows into a roaring fire. The fuel? Arguing and wanting to get even or spreading rumors about someone. Suddenly, like a wildfire whipped by the wind, the damage done to others becomes serious. Reputations are ruined, and in the case of anger, violence flares up and someone is hurt or killed. Things can escalate quickly. The image of the flame is a good one. Without adding wood to a small fire, it will die out and turn to ashes. But throw on a couple logs, and the fire will grow larger. Keep feeding it, and soon it will be a blazing fire. That can be a wonderful thing in the middle of the dark woods on a chilly evening, but if it gets out of control, it is very difficult to stop. So it is with anger and violence, and so it is with rumors and gossip. Put out those flames as soon as you can.

Think About . . .

Reflect on fire and how similar it is to our own emotions. How can both be positive as well as negative forces?

Today's Scripture Passage
Sirach, Chapter 29

What do we really need to live? What are the basic necessities of life? Verse 21 sums it up simply: water, food, clothing, and a home. And really, what else is there? Isn't it true that everything else we get is simply a variation on these four basics? We need to remember that for so many people in the world, these four basic necessities, which we easily take for granted, are things they struggle for. So many people in the world spend so much of their time and energy scraping together enough food and water to make it through another day. Some of them don't have a home and have very little clothing. But we know that all human beings have a God-given right to have these needs met. Our obligation as well-fed people who live in homes with so many conveniences is to remember our brothers and sisters that have so little.

Think About . . .

What can you do today to help someone with the basic necessities of life?

Today's Scripture Passage
Sirach, Chapter 30

There was a song a few years back called "Don't Worry, Be Happy." It was an upbeat song with a catchy tune. And actually that pretty much sums up the message of verse 23. What good can we achieve by worrying? It doesn't do any good at all and can even be harmful. Ben Sira says it can cause death, which is probably not too far off base. If you get consumed by worry, it will eat you up. People who enjoy life and don't get caught up in worrying seem a lot better off. Think about it. How can worrying about an upcoming test help you pass it? Studying and resting do that. How does worrying about a health concern help you? Seeing a doctor does that. Many of us get so caught up on the worry treadmill that it can wear us down. Ben Sira urges us to not let ourselves worry and to strive rather for happiness. A positive attitude can work wonders.

Think About . . .

What are you worried about right now? Why?

Today's Scripture Passage
Sirach, Chapter 31

You are invited to a nice dinner party. How should you behave? It would be hard to find a more practical guide to appropriate behavior than in verses 12–31. The advice has certainly stood the test of time. The key phrase is verse 22: In everything you do, practice moderation. Don't get carried away. In other words, don't eat too much, don't talk too loud, and especially don't drink too much. The old-fashioned word is *etiquette*. It seems to be a dying art, but it was once taught in schools. It refers to the art of polite behavior and covers everything from how to correctly use silverware at a banquet to how to converse with the people around you. Depending on your background, you may know a lot of this already. If not, then Ben Sira's advice is a good place to start.

Think About . . .

Reflect on times when you have felt awkward in a formal social setting. What did you learn by observing others?

Today's Scripture Passage
Sirach, Chapter 32

The last words of this chapter are perhaps the wisest of all: Trust in God and you cannot lose. So much of the advice in this chapter is very practical and makes a lot of sense. Verse 19 counsels us to always think things through before acting. Verse 21 advises us not to be too sure of ourselves, even if it looks like clear sailing ahead. Verse 23 tells us to always be careful. This is all stuff we have heard before, but when it is put in the context of trusting God and being a person of faith, it makes even more sense. To become wise is to deepen our faith and to know that God will provide for us, that God walks with us. But we also need to be sensible people who strive to make good decisions and to be grateful for God's guidance and gifts.

Think About . . .

What are you struggling with right now? Think it through, pray about it, and be assured of God's presence and guidance as you discern.

Today's Scripture Passage
Sirach, Chapter 33

For centuries of human history, slavery was an accepted part of life. All the great civilizations allowed some form of slavery, including our own up to 1865. Now we look back sadly at the reality of slavery and realize how wrong and sinful it is to buy and sell human beings. Part of the problem with slavery is that it is easy to find justification for it in the Bible. It occurs in several places. Verses 24–31 are perfect examples. There is not a word about the evil of slavery. This awareness has occurred gradually as we discern where God is calling us. No committed Christian today would find slavery acceptable or moral. Why not? God has revealed to us through time that it is wrong.

Think About . . .

Why is it so important to understand that the Bible is not an answer book?

Today's Scripture Passage
Sirach, Chapter 34

Travel agents must love verses 9–12, which serve as a great ad for the benefits of taking a trip. A person who is well traveled gains a lot of experience and learns much. Traveling to new places, especially internationally, is one of the best ways to learn. Traveling teaches you that there is more than one way to live, that every group of people has its own culture. The experience of traveling and seeing different ways of doing things is enriching. More and more colleges offer study-abroad programs, which encourage students to use the world as a textbook and to integrate those experiences into their lives. There are so many places to go and things to see in our diverse world, and all of it is part of God's creative plan for us. Another great lesson in traveling often is that we learn to travel light, which is a good way to go through life as well!

Think About . . .

If you could travel anywhere in the world next month, where would you go and why?

Today's Scripture Passage
Sirach, Chapter 35

There are two striking lines in this chapter. One is verse 9, which speaks of giving to God as generously as you are able because God has given so much to you. The other, verse 12, states that God is a God of justice who shows no favorites. (These verses may be slightly different, depending on your translation). Both messages are important. How can we fail to be generous to God when we have been given so much? There are many ways of giving back to God, but the most obvious is to share the wealth we have. It may not be much, but we can always spare something for others and for our church. And it's always good to remember that God does not show favorites. It may seem that way at times, like some people get all the breaks. But it's foolish to apply our understanding of fairness to God. We don't know the mind of God, but we do believe that God loves us all, no matter what.

Think About . . .

How can you be more generous to God?

Today's Scripture Passage
Sirach, Chapter 36

In the prayer that encompasses verses 1–17, one passage proves disturbing. In verses 6–8, Ben Sira prays that God will get angry enough to bring down Israel's enemies and wipe out their rulers. This is the sort of talk we are used to hearing at pep rallies when we are trying to rouse up some school spirit. But isn't God supposed to love everyone? Aren't we supposed to love everyone? Didn't Jesus tell us to love our enemies and pray for our persecutors? Yes, he did, but remember that Sirach reflects an earlier theology that predates Jesus. In the writer's eyes, justice is accomplished when we win and our enemies lose. It's a lot more complicated than that in reality. It would be rare today to encounter someone who prays aloud for God to punish our nation's enemies. We think differently, right?

Think About . . .

Think about whom we consider the current enemies of our nation. Take a moment to pray for them, especially their leaders.

Today's Scripture Passage
Sirach, Chapter 37

A few chapters ago, we read a section that seemed like it was written by travel agents. Verses 27–31 could make a dietician's day! They provide practical advice on eating. Our society is concerned about obesity, and rightly so, as too many of us eat way too much for our own good. Clearly, however, the problem also existed in biblical times. Ben Sira advises his readers to keep their appetites under control and avoid foods that disagree with them. By eating too much and too often, we endanger our lives. Cool it, in other words. Eat to live rather than live to eat, as the saying goes. Food is everywhere, and a lot of us eat foods that aren't good for us. Why end up having to pay big bucks for a special diet program? Why not just cut back and watch what you eat every day? Make healthy choices.

Think About . . .

Reflect on your own eating habits. Are they healthy?

Today's Scripture Passage
Sirach, Chapter 38

Now comes high praise and affirmation for the workers of the world, especially those involved in skilled labor. Ben Sira talks about scholars or scribes, those who plow, engravers and designers, metal workers, and potters. Without these hard-working people, we would not have towns and cities. Today we might add maintenance workers, builders, contractors, police officers, and so many others who make a city work. Hard work is a good thing because it helps cities stay alive and fosters economic growth. There are so many career choices out there. We each need to turn to God and ask direction. Our natural gifts generally point us in a certain direction, and learning skills or earning a degree prepares us to contribute to society. The last verse is a beautiful tribute to what good hard work accomplishes—it maintains the fabric of the world.

Think About . . .

How do you benefit from the hard work of others each day?

Today's Scripture Passage
Sirach, Chapter 39

What's going on? Why is this happening? In verses 16–17 and 21, Ben Sira points out that there is simply no need to ask these questions. For a believer, all things are created for a purpose, even though we can't figure it out right now. And whatever God created is good. Everything has its purpose and time, a similar thought to that expressed in the Book of Ecclesiastes, chapter 3. And here's a key point, which we can so easily forget: Everything God commands will be done in its own time. When is that, we ask? We do not know, but rest assured, it will happen. It's just that God has a different perspective than we do. God's frame of reference, after all, is eternity. Things don't just happen. Everything has a design and a purpose. As people of faith, we trust that to be true, knowing that it doesn't always make sense to us.

Think About . . .

What are some of the things happening in your life that don't make a lot of sense right now? Can you see how they might some day?

Today's Scripture Passage
Sirach, Chapter 40

What brings joy in life? Verses 18–27 contain a poem listing ten pairs of joys, which, as good as they are, are then surpassed by something else. All ten have this same structure, which gives them a poetic feel. Look at them carefully. There are almost thirty things listed that can be counted as joys in life. It almost reads like a game. Well, wine and music are great, but, hey, the love of your friends is even better. Gold and silver are pretty cool, but good advice is even better. Being rich and strong can make us confident, but respecting and reverencing God is so much better. That one is saved for last, by the way. Recall that to be truly wise is to have a deep reverence for God. Yes, as Ben Sira points out, it is like a garden of blessings.

Think About . . .

Take a moment to list all the joys in your life. Don't forget to think of what is even better, as Ben Sira does. Have fun doing this, and thank God for all the joys!

Today's Scripture Passage
Sirach, Chapter 41

"We're all gonna die!" Well, that's the truth isn't it? We know that, even though we may not like to think about it much. There is a lot of wisdom in Ben Sira's words in verses 1–3. For someone in the prime of life, death is very unwelcome. For someone who is old or sick or both, death can be a welcome relief. Don't be afraid of it; it will come to all those older than you as well as all those younger. That's the way of it. The one certainty about life is that it will end, sooner for some than we'd like. Don't be scared of death. Cartoonists tend to portray death as a hooded figure dressed in black and carrying a huge scythe. Not a very welcoming image! Why not envision death as a bright angel smiling and holding out a hand to you? Try it!

Think About . . .

What do you hope to accomplish before you die? Make a list of twenty-five things. Tuck it away somewhere for future reference.

Today's Scripture Passage
Sirach, Chapter 42

It's not easy being a father to daughters, especially when they are teenagers. It's true now, and clearly it was true in the time of Ben Sira. A lot of dads today would probably agree with much of what is said in verses 9–14. There's a lot to worry about! We know that Ben Sira's attitude toward women would be considered sexist today, but we also need to realize that behind all of his statements is one very significant truth: Most fathers love their daughters very much. And because of that, they want to protect them from harm. Sometimes fathers can become overprotective, which can cause problems. Whenever you struggle with your parents or guardians, remind yourself that they really are acting out of a genuine concern for you. They care deeply about what happens to you. That's true for sons as well as daughters. Your parents or guardians are trying their best!

Think About . . .

What is the biggest struggle you have with your parents or guardians? Try to see things from their perspective. What do you see?

Today's Scripture Passage
Sirach, Chapter 43

Ben Sira is clearly at his poetic best in this chapter, which is a continuation of the last part of chapter 42. With eloquent language, he describes the works of God in nature. In verses 11–12, for example, he describes the beauty of a rainbow. In verse 28, he begins the concluding section by urging us to praise God for God's majesty and splendor. He also reminds us that as wonderful as all God's works are, we must realize that there is so much more to God than we can perceive. We are seeing only a fraction of God's goodness. We really have no idea how much more there is to God. It is this element of mystery and majesty, as well as knowing that there is so much more to life than what meets the eye, that makes God so fascinating to us. Our God is an awesome God. That's what this chapter is all about.

Think About . . .

What part of nature most reveals God to you? Why?

Today's Scripture Passage
Sirach, Chapter 44

For the next six chapters, Ben Sira sings the praises of "godly men," as he describes them. He begins by praising what they have done, and in verses 9–15, he also remembers all those whose names are long forgotten but who nevertheless live on in their offspring. He then begins a list of the early patriarchs and includes Noah, Abraham, Isaac, and Jacob, some of the "stars" of the Book of Genesis. These are the heroes of our faith, and it is appropriate that Ben Sira finishes his book by proclaiming their names and deeds. These are the people who lived lives of faithfulness to God. As we know, they were all human with the usual virtues and vices, but they lived out the covenant and passed down the faith to us. In the Catholic Tradition, we continue that list with lots of saints down through the present day. What a legacy!

Think About . . .

Whom might you identify as unsung heroes in your neighborhood or community?

Today's Scripture Passage
Sirach, Chapter 45

This chapter focuses on Moses, Aaron, and Phinehas. Ben Sira devotes seventeen verses to Aaron and only five to Moses. Phinehas is a descendant of Aaron. Scholars tell us that Ben Sira seems to be singling out Aaron because Aaron's line began the tradition of the Jewish priesthood. Much of what Ben Sira describes about Aaron are the vestments and accessories of the priesthood, which, by the time of Ben Sira, had become quite ornate. Unlike many of the patriarchs, Aaron's inheritance is not in land but in the priesthood, which passes from father to son. While we as Christians focus on the calling of the priesthood, in the days before Christ, it was an inherited profession. If your dad was a priest, then you would be too. Of course, that was true of most professions in biblical times, whether you were a shepherd, a fisherman, or a carpenter.

Think About . . .

Do you see yourself following in the same profession as your parents or guardians? Why or why not?

Today's Scripture Passage
Sirach, Chapter 46

Form verse 11 through the end of the chapter, Ben Sira discusses the judges, ending with Samuel. The term *judges* as it is used here does not refer to the kind of judges we are used to today. These judges are primarily military leaders who come forth most often when the Israelites are under attack. They unite the people against the common enemy. The stories of the judges are told in the book of the same name. The great Samuel is the bridge between the judges and the prophets. We know him as the one who anoints both Saul and David as kings. He is known for his integrity. Recall that one of Saul's last acts is to call up the ghost of Samuel to find out what will happen to him. As verse 20 explains, even in death, Samuel's wisdom is sought.

Think About . . .

What does the word *integrity* mean to you? Name some people you know that have integrity.

Today's Scripture Passage
Sirach, Chapter 47

Ben Sira now pays tribute to the two most famous kings of Israel, David and Solomon. He certainly praises the great King David, but he does not mention his faults. The same is not true for Solomon, however. David's son does not fare as well as his father, even though he has so much going for him. His wisdom is legendary, yet he is not smart enough to realize that by building temples for the god of his many foreign wives, he is violating the first commandment. Ben Sira points out well the rise and fall of King Solomon. After Solomon the kingdom splits in two, and never again does it achieve the glory days it knew under David and Solomon. In fact, after Solomon things go downhill pretty quickly, which eventually leads to the time of Jeremiah and the Exile.

Think About . . .

How is it possible for a wise person to be a fool?

Today's Scripture Passage
Sirach, Chapter 48

Three prophets and one king. That's what this chapter is about. Ben Sira praises the three famous prophets, Elijah, Elisha, and Isaiah. Hezekiah was king while Isaiah prophesied, and Hezekiah clearly followed the guidance of Isaiah. Let's recall the role of the prophets. It is not so much to foretell the future, although they do some of that; rather, it is the far more challenging task of calling the people and the rulers to be faithful to God. The main prophetic message is very much like the one we receive with ashes on the first day of Lent: "Turn away from sin and be faithful to the gospel" (*Sacramentary*, p. 77). That's it. Each prophet has his own way of communicating that message. Recall some of the creative ways Jeremiah makes his points. Prophets are generally proven to be true prophets after they die. Are there any prophets being ignored today?

Think About . . .

What prophetic messages have you heard lately?

Today's Scripture Passage
Sirach, Chapter 49

Verse 10 refers to the bones of the twelve prophets giving life to others. It is an interesting idea, because the early Christians took that notion quite literally. When followers of Christ were martyred, their remains were treated with profound respect. This evolved into the devotion centered on relics, which often meant pieces of the bones of these early Christians. Eventually relics became a big deal in the Church, especially in the Middle Ages, when it was a mark of status for a church to have the relics of a particular saint. Relics are still part of Church practice, but it's important to recall why. Relics are believed to be holy objects because the good people they were part of are now saints and so, similar to the thought expressed by Ben Sira, they can be a source of life and inspiration.

Think About . . .

What items do you or your family members possess that were owned by a relative or friend who has died? Why are these items meaningful?

Today's Scripture Passage
Sirach, Chapter 50

Ben Sira spends most of this chapter praising Simon, the son of Jochanan, who is high priest during Ben Sira's lifetime. Clearly Ben Sira has a profound respect for Simon. He provides a detailed list of his accomplishments, especially his majestic appearance as he performs the ritual sacrifice in the Temple. It is a reminder that the tradition of the priesthood comes from Judaism, although it is ironic that there are no priests in Judaism today. The Romans' destruction of the Temple in Jerusalem in AD 70 effectively ended the role of the priesthood because they offered sacrifice in the Temple. One priest was appointed High Priest, and he would preside over the other priests and the Temple rituals. The Gospels tell us that Caiaphas was the high priest at the time of Jesus's Crucifixion.

Think About . . .

Reflect on the role of priests in Christianity today and the unique challenges and rewards of their calling.

Today's Scripture Passage
Sirach, Chapter 51

This chapter brings to a close the Book of Sirach. Verse 23 refers to "the house of instruction," which leads many scholars to conclude that Ben Sira actually led a school. It makes sense when we look back at how the book is arranged. It is clearly divided into "teaching units" that could serve as daily lessons. It also makes sense that at some point, Ben Sira would want to record all of this in a book so it would not be lost. By ending with a historical look at the heroic figures of the Old Testament, it almost seems like a review of all the wisdom of the ages to the time of the author. It is a blessing to have this collected in one book. Sirach is one of the deuterocanonical books of the Bible, which means it is an accepted part of the Bible for Catholics but not for most Protestants, who refer to this book and a few others as apocryphal.

Think About . . .

What wisdom of Sirach have you found most valuable or thought provoking?

Today's Scripture Passage
Joshua, Chapter 1

The Book of Joshua follows the Pentateuch, or To-rah, which comprise the first five books of the Bi-ble. Joshua is the first in a series of books that are called the historical books. They conclude with 2 Maccabees, and include the books of 1 and 2 Samuel. The Pentateuch ends with the death of Moses. His successor is Joshua, who is told by the Lord in verses 2–3 to prepare to cross the Jordan River and enter the Promised Land. Recall that this is the land promised to Abraham so long ago. The events in the Book of Joshua occur from about 1250 to 1200 BC. David ruled around the year 1000 BC, to give you a historical perspective. The clause "Be firm and steadfast" occurs twice in the first chapter. The people must follow the Law of God as spelled out in the Torah. If they do so, the Promised Land will become theirs.

Think About . . .

Reflect on times you have remained firm and steadfast about something. When have you done the opposite?

Today's Scripture Passage

Joshua, Chapter 2

The story of Joshua and the conquest of Canaan is filled with intrigue. Here, thanks to the kindness of a woman named Rahab, the lives of two Hebrew spies are saved. In turn, Rahab asks for a favor from the Israelites. When they take over the land, she asks that her family members be spared. The two Israelites heartily agree to her request. And so Rahab hides them and then later lets them out of the city by lowering them down the wall on a rope. Off they go, no doubt singing the praises of Rahab. What motivates Rahab to risk her life and save the Israelites? Could it be the same courage that inspired so many people to provide hiding places for the Jews during the Nazi regime? The big news the spies bring back to Joshua, news they learn from Rahab, is that everyone is afraid of the Israelites.

Think About . . .

Where do people find the courage to risk their lives and livelihood to save the lives of others?

Today's Scripture Passage
Joshua, Chapter 3

Crossing the Jordan River is a key moment for the Israelites. They are officially entering the Promised Land. The priests lead the way, carrying the ark of the Covenant, the holiest object of Judaism. All the people are instructed to follow. When the priests wade into the Jordan, the water disappears so everyone can cross. What is the significance of this event? You probably know the story of the Israelites' crossing the Red Sea. Think about what happened. The waters parted until all the people passed through. The same thing happens here, and this miraculous event is meant to parallel that one. In both cases, God is with the people to deliver them safely. This crossing is a sign to a new generation that God is with them, because everyone who was part of the crossing of the Red Sea has since died.

Think About . . .

Where do you see God's power in your life?

Today's Scripture Passage
Joshua, Chapter 4

This chapter repeats some of the story elements of the previous chapter, which most likely are two or more separate traditions brought together. A few key elements in this story are about the memorial stones. Of course there are to be twelve stones to represent the Twelve Tribes of Israel. They are placed in a circle, which is the meaning of Gilgal. Verse 19 tells us the date of these events—the tenth day of the first month. For us this would be January, but for the Israelites at this time, it is the month of *Nisan*, which occurs in what we call March and April. The Israelites of this time follow a lunar calendar, as do the Jews and Muslims today. This is the time of Passover, so the crossing of the Jordan takes on even more significance because of the holy Passover season. All this is to depict Joshua as the new Moses, who is leading his people to freedom.

Think About . . .

Whom do we see as the new Moses and why?

Today's Scripture Passage
Joshua, Chapter 5

Circumcision is the sign of the covenant required of all Jewish males. It is so basic and fundamental a sign of the covenant that Joshua needs to make sure the Israelites conform to the Law before they begin to conquer the Land of Canaan and before they celebrate the ritual of Passover. The requirement of circumcision applies to all Jewish males to this day. This new generation that was not part of the crossing of the Red Sea, but that was born in the forty years since, is required to fulfill this mandate. Recall how this was also a pivotal issue for the early Christians as they expanded into the Gentile world (see the Acts of the Apostles, chapter 15). The early Church decided that non-Jewish Christians did not need to be circumcised. The events in this chapter help us understand why this was such a big step to take.

Think About . . .

Every religion has some sort of defining ritual. What is the sign for Christians, and why is it significant?

Today's Scripture Passage
Joshua, Chapter 6

Joshua fights the battle of Jericho, and the walls come tumbling down. That pretty much sums up this chapter, as we read about the first of many battles the Israelites fight to gain possession of the Promised Land. What really happened? We don't know, but chances are the stories of the battle of Jericho were told and retold so many times, that eventually we ended up with this very ritualistic and miraculous account. Archaeologists have concluded that Jericho was probably already in ruins when the Israelites got to the town. No matter. The religious truth is what counts here: God is with the people; therefore, for them, and for us, walls come tumbling down. With God on our side, so many kinds of walls can fall down before us. We gain courage when we know God is with us.

Think About . . .

What walls have come tumbling down in your own life because of your relationship with God?

Today's Scripture Passage
Joshua, Chapter 7

We need to remember that when God puts a conquered city under a ban, no one can take away anything from the city; in other words, no one has the right to derive any gain from the conquest. The Israelites are defeated at Ai, and Joshua can't figure out what's going on. Why would God lead them to the Promised Land only to have their enemies defeat them? As it turns out, the issue is one of obedience. Someone violated the sacred ban; that is, someone disobeyed God's orders. That person is Achor, from the Tribe of Judah. In what may seem like a cruel action, especially because he readily confessed his sin, Achor is taken into a valley and stoned to death. Again this is a lesson about obedience.

Think About . . .

Why do you think obedience is such an important part of early Israelite history?

Today's Scripture Passage
Joshua, Chapter 8

What didn't happen in the previous chapter due to Achor's sin now happens here. Ai is completely destroyed. Notice how military strategy plays a key role as the soldiers of Ai are lured out of the city by what appears to be fleeing Israelite troops. In reality the enemy soldiers are being led into a clever trap and are quickly ambushed by the Israelites. Like Jericho before it, Ai is annihilated as the Israelites begin to reclaim the land promised to them. It is hard for us to read that twelve thousand men and women of Ai are slaughtered that day. It seems so senseless and barbaric to us, but we have very different rules and understanding about how noncombatants should be treated. These are commonly called the Geneva Conventions, which lay out generally agreed upon principles about how war should be conducted in a "civilized" manner, which is ironic in itself.

Think About . . .

Do you think civilization has changed for the better or for the worse since the time of Joshua?

Today's Scripture Passage
Joshua, Chapter 9

This chapter is about trust and deception. The Gibeonites decide that rather than fighting the Israelites, they will attempt to negotiate with them. The only problem is that their negotiating is based on deception. Because the Israelites have been commanded to destroy their enemies, they are forbidden to make treaties with them. The Gibeonites know this, so they assume disguises and claim to be from some far-off land, saying they have heard about the mighty God of the Israelites and want to serve this God. The leaders fall for it and form an alliance that is sealed with an oath. When the Israelites later find out that they have been duped, they can't do anything about it. They have sworn an oath. Though it is true that the Gibeonites deliberately deceive the Israelites, it is also true that the Israelite leaders do not seek the Lord's help in deciding what to do. Therefore, they also violate a trust.

Think About . . .

Reflect on the importance of prayer and reflection before making a big decision.

Today's Scripture Passage
Joshua, Chapter 10

Two miraculous events are described in verses 11–14. One is a severe hailstorm that killed many of the Amorites. The other is that the sun stood still for an entire day. Though it is easy to conceive how a hailstorm with large pieces of hail could kill people, it is harder for us, in the twenty-first century, to believe that the sun actually stopped in the sky. Science informs us that the sun doesn't move in the first place, information unknown to ancient peoples. Today we would say that the earth stopped spinning, which is also hard to believe. Again, as in so many places in the Old Testament, this is meant to show who is really in charge. It is God, not the Israelites, who is responsible for the Israelites' victories. The description of the sun standing still makes that clear.

Think About . . .

Recall an instance when you felt as if time were standing still or moving very slowly.

Today's Scripture Passage
Joshua, Chapter 11

Two telling passages in this chapter help put everything in context. The first is verse 15, which clearly states that Joshua is carrying out the command of Moses, who is carrying out the command of God, so as to leave no doubt that Joshua is acting in accordance with the will of God. This underlines the reason for his success. The second passage is verse 18, which says that all these wars lasted a long time. Because so much seems to happen so quickly in these chapters, it's easy to see the whole campaign as a set of dominoes collapsing. It is much more complicated and messy than that. Verse 18 reminds us of that fact. Yes, God is with Joshua, but it also takes a long time to complete the conquest of a land filled with so many tribes of Canaanites.

Think About . . .

When God is with us and we are with God, we will be victorious. What does this mean in your own life?

Today's Scripture Passage
Joshua, Chapter 12

This chapter brings to a close the stories of the conquest of Canaan. It all seems to happen so quickly and so smoothly that we need to remind ourselves, as pointed out in the last chapter, that this simply is not the case. Keep in mind the roles of storytelling and oral tradition in shaping a narrative. This chapter provides a list of all the lands and kings that are conquered by Joshua. The Israelites do indeed eventually take over the Land of Canaan, but as we shall see as we continue reading the Book of Joshua, more skirmishes and battles take place. What most likely happens, as we have learned through archaeology, is that the conquest of Canaan is a combination of battles and infiltration. As the Israelites grow and prosper, their sheer numbers work in their favor. Yes, the Promised Land becomes the home of the Israelites, but it definitely does not happen overnight.

Think About . . .

Patience is a virtue many of us struggle with. Why is it so hard for us to be patient?

Today's Scripture Passage
Joshua, Chapter 13

The next few chapters may get a bid tedious to plow through. As is typical in Old Testament writing, the author gets specific about which tribe gets which territory and what the boundaries are. County land offices today perform much the same function, except they use specific maps and technology to determine property lines and ownership boundaries. Twice in this chapter, it is explained that the Tribe of Levi received no land. The reason is that the Levites became the priestly class. A male born into the tribe of Levi inherited the power of the priesthood, not land. We are reminded again of how differently we view priesthood as Catholics and Christians. People feel called to this profession, not born into it. The very fact that in the Roman Catholic Tradition, priests are celibate ensures that the priesthood will not pass from father to son.

Think About . . .

Why is owning land and property so important in our society?

Today's Scripture Passage
Joshua, Chapter 14

The story of Caleb is about the rewards of loyalty. Caleb reminds Joshua of what both of them were told by Moses (see Numbers 13:30–33 and 14:24). Moses was impressed with Caleb's loyalty and promised him he would be given land for a heritage. Joshua is true to the promise and gives Hebron, an important place in biblical history, to Caleb. Sarah dies and is buried there (see Genesis 23:1–7), and later David first rules from there (see 2 Samuel 5:3-5). Hebron plays a strategic role in the history of Israel. This story is a reminder that loyalty pays off—in this case, quite literally. To be loyal means to stick by someone and to prove yourself dependable and reliable. This is what Caleb does, and for that he is rewarded, despite his age of eighty-five.

Think About . . .

What examples of loyalty can you recall from the Bible or history? How have you experienced loyalty in your own life?

Today's Scripture Passage
Joshua, Chapter 15

Notice what city falls within the boundaries of the Tribe of Judah: Ephrathah, or Bethlehem. This is the city David comes from and where Jesus will be born, one thousand years after David. Judah therefore becomes the preeminent tribe and eventually gives its name to both the land of Judea as well as to the religion of Judaism. The one city that becomes key for the Jews is Jerusalem, but remember that it is David who finally conquers the Jebusites and claims the city as the capital of his new kingdom as well as the site of the Temple. Notice how in this list, Bethlehem is simply one of many cities mentioned. It is only later in biblical history that it gains prominence as the birthplace of the greatest king of Israel and of the Messiah.

Think About . . .

It is possible that one day you or a classmate could help bring fame to your city. Imagine how that might happen.

Today's Scripture Passage
Joshua, Chapter 16

Recall that Joseph's two sons are named Ephraim and Manasseh. They receive a special blessing from their grandfather Jacob (see Genesis, chapter 48). There is no tribe of Joseph; rather there are tribes named Ephraim and Manasseh. Appropriately these two tribes border one another and occupy the middle ground between what is known today as the Sea of Galilee in the north and the Dead Sea in the south. Neither of these bodies of water is technically a sea; *lake* is a more appropriate term, given their size. The Jordan River connects these two bodies of water and serves as a border for modern-day Israel. The Jordan River plays a key role in the life of Jesus, as this is where John baptizes him.

Think About . . .

Take a moment to pray for the Holy Land, spiritual home to Jews, Christians, and Muslims.

Today's Scripture Passage
Joshua, Chapter 17

What the two Joseph tribes are complaining to Joshua about are probably very real limitations. In the valley, the Canaanites have iron chariots, which are difficult to defeat because the two clans of Ephraim and Manasseh do not have chariots. And the mountains are heavily wooded, so the actual land they can occupy is tight for so many people. Joshua gives them practical advice: cut down the trees so you can settle in the mountains, and work on defeating the Canaanites. Obviously the second will be harder to accomplish than the first, but these tribes have numbers on their side, so it can be done. Clearly Joshua is highly regarded for his military and strategic skills as well as just plain common sense. He is a worthy and able successor to Moses.

Think About . . .

Who in your life is a source of common sense? Whom can you go to in order to figure out what to do next?

Today's Scripture Passage
Joshua, Chapter 18

Now the focus of attention is on Shiloh, which served as the chief center of worship before Jerusalem. It is also centrally located, so it has symbolic significance for the notion that the Lord is in the midst of the Lord's people. Shiloh is where Samuel was raised (see 1 Samuel, chapters 1–3). Seven tribes have yet to have land allotted to them. Again we are reminded that the land has to be fought for. Scouts are sent out to survey the land to give Joshua some idea of the terrain and cities yet to be settled. The method used to distribute land to the tribes is to draw lots. It may seem random to us, but in biblical times, drawing lots in a prayerful setting is considered as a holy expression of God's will rather than mere chance. This occurs several times in the Bible, including choosing an Apostle to take the place of Judas (see the Acts of the Apostles 1:26).

Think About . . .

Do you think God's will can be expressed by drawing straws or guessing the right number? Why or why not?

Today's Scripture Passage
Joshua, Chapter 19

An interesting thing happens to the Tribe of Simeon. The land allotted to this tribe lies within the land of the Tribe of Judah. In fact, it is in an area called the Negeb, which is basically a wilderness. The truth is that early on the Simeonites disappear. It is not clear what happens to them, but when Jacob delivers his blessing to each of his sons, he says that both Levi and Simeon's descendants will be scattered throughout the land (see Genesis 49:5–7), which seems to acknowledge the fact that the identity of the Tribe of Simeon is lost. However, it is important to the story and symbolic to keep the listing of the Twelve Tribes of Israel. By the time of King Solomon, however, the tribes have lost their territorial significance and are used only to trace ancestry or genealogy.

Think About . . .

American Indians retain the designation of tribes and clans to describe themselves. How many tribes can you name? Are there any in your area?

Today's Scripture Passage
Joshua, Chapter 20

This brief chapter contains an important option for someone who has accidentally caused the death of another. Six cities of refuge, or asylum, are set apart for people to seek sanctuary. Ordinarily if someone kills someone else, the killer's life would be taken to balance out the crime. However, because an unintentional killing is not murder, the one who has committed homicide may flee to the gates of these cities of refuge for safety from blood revenge. This establishes an important principle of asylum, which is actually spelled out in two other places (see Numbers 35:9–28 and Deuteronomy 19:1–13). With the death of the high priest, the killer can return home. This is probably to put a time limit on the sanctuary provision. As we know, we have hundreds of thousands of refugees in our world today. All of them are seeking some sort of asylum.

Think About . . .

What refugees are you aware of in your own community or area? Why have they fled their homeland?

Today's Scripture Passage
Joshua, Chapter 21

This chapter serves as a sort of twin to the last one. This time forty-eight cities are given to the Levites. Recall that as part of the priestly class, the Levites were not given land of their own. The cities and pastures they receive provide some economic security but still allow them to serve as priests (often descendants of Aaron, the brother of Moses) or to be part of the rites of worship, somewhat like deacons today in the Catholic Church. The chapter ends by summing up all that has happened since the beginning of the Book of Joshua. As promised by God, the Israelites now successfully occupy the Land of Canaan, the Promised Land. God has been true to God's word. All the promises have been fulfilled.

Think About . . .

Take a moment to reflect on the ministry of priesthood. It is a challenging one. Pray for the priests you know, that they can persevere in their calling to serve the people of God.

Today's Scripture Passage
Joshua, Chapter 22

What we have here is a combination of geography and politics in a religious context. The tribes east of the Jordan River—Reuben, Gad, and Manasseh—are now free to return to their lands after having helped the other tribes complete their conquest of Canaan. These eastern tribes then decide to build a huge altar near the Jordan River. Why are the other tribes so upset? This act is seen as a threat to the religious and political unity of the Israelites, sort of like seceding from the union. If this is accurate, a civil war could ensue. However, the eastern tribes reassure the others that their primary intent is to let the altar serve as a witness to their children that they also are part of the Chosen People. They do not plan to offer sacrifices on it; rather, it will serve as a reminder. The altar is thus named "witness" in Hebrew. Dispute settled.

Think About . . .

What reminders do you have in your room or home that witness to your faith?

Today's Scripture Passage
Joshua, Chapter 23

Joshua, now an old man, gives the people his farewell speech. The message is a familiar one: "God has fulfilled all of God's promises to you. You in turn must remain faithful to God. If you do not, then the land will be taken away from you." The requirements are clear: stay obedient and faithful, and everything will go your way; disobey and sin, and you will fail. It is hard for us to view God in quite the same way. We are much more aware of the grayness and messiness of life. Many people who are faithful and do all the right things end up suffering great losses, while some wicked and careless people seem to prosper. The Book of Job struggles with the issue of bad things happening to good people. At this point early in the Israelites' history, God's relationship with them is very much like that of a strict loving parent who does not hesitate to punish. Jesus eventually reveals a very different image of God.

Think About . . .

How do you know you are doing God's will?

Today's Scripture Passage
Joshua, Chapter 24

This final chapter gives us what seems like a second farewell speech. Here Joshua reminds the people of their history. It is so important to tell the story over and over again. Joshua urges the people to reject idols and false gods, a constant temptation. The people renew their covenant with God. Verse 24 sums up their response: We promise to stay faithful to God. The Book of Joshua is a simplified version of the Israelites' long and painful struggle to take over the land that was given them so long ago. After Joshua comes the Book of Judges, which covers the next two hundred years of Israel's history. Then comes the time of the monarchy, beginning with 1 Samuel, chapters 1 and 2. Joshua has proven himself a worthy successor to Moses. Through it all, he remains a faithful servant of God and an excellent leader of his people. Add him to your list of biblical heroes.

Think About . . .

What is your favorite Old Testament story or book? Why?

Today's Scripture Passage
1 Timothy, Chapter 1

The final books we will explore are 1 and 2 Timothy. Along with the Book of Titus, which follows, they are referred to as the Pastoral Letters because so much of their focus is on pastoral matters within the newly established churches. You may recall that Timothy was one of Paul's closest companions and an associate, which is also clear from verse 2. Chapter 16 of the Acts of the Apostles describes their meeting in Lystra. Timothy plays a key role in establishing and caring for the Church in Corinth. These books serve as an encouragement and guide to young Timothy. Verse 19 describes faith and a good conscience, two attributes that make Timothy such a trusted leader. Think about what a blessing it is to possess both of those traits. Clearly Paul recognizes that Timothy's gifts will serve him well in caring for the first Christians.

Think About . . .

How strong and solid would you rate your faith and conscience?

Today's Scripture Passage
1 Timothy, Chapter 2

Once again we encounter what we would call sexist attitudes toward women. Verses 9–15 basically state that women should be seen and not heard. The prevailing attitude toward women at this time is that they are inferior to men and not as capable of deep thought. In biblical times, a woman certainly cannot hold authority over a man. The writer of the letter, possibly Paul, resorts to the story of Adam and Eve to say that Eve was the one, after all, who was deceived, not Adam. We believe today that God is calling us all to a more respectful and holistic approach to our faith and a deeper awareness of the value of both women and men. Women do serve as teachers and managers of men. The world has not ended. The Catholic Church has named several women as doctors of the Church, which means they are saintly teachers. Thank God they didn't heed the advice given in this chapter!

Think About . . .

How does sexism show a lack of respect?

Today's Scripture Passage
1 Timothy, Chapter 3

You might be a bit surprised at the advice given about bishops and deacons in this chapter. Both are to be married only once and are to manage their children and households well. Verse 11 talks about women deacons, although some would interpret this passage as referring to the wives of deacons. Historical evidence shows that women did serve in leadership roles in the early Church. This passage is a reminder to us that the Church has evolved over the centuries. The tradition of male priestly celibacy developed gradually. Today in the Roman Catholic Church, there are married deacons but no married bishops and no female deacons. The Catholic faith is based on revelation from both the Scriptures and Tradition. That reality continues to guide the Church as it responds to an ever-changing world. Where is the Holy Spirit leading us? Time will tell.

Think About . . .

Why is it valuable to rely on both the Scriptures and Tradition as guides?

Today's Scripture Passage
1 Timothy, Chapter 4

Verse 12 contains a powerful message for you. Just because you're young, don't let anyone dismiss you. You can actually be an example for others in how you speak, act, and live out your faith. A lot of people stereotype teenagers as loud, self-centered, and reckless. You can prove them wrong, and that's exactly what the author of this letter is advising Timothy. Your youthful energy combined with a growing faith means you have much to offer to your church and our world. Recall that God called Jeremiah and Samuel when they were young, and David was anointed at a young age. So your youth can serve you well! Speak up and get involved. Let others know you are a follower of Christ by how you live. Set an example, blaze a trail, and do it all for God.

Think About . . .

How can you be a stronger witness to your faith?

Today's Scripture Passage
1 Timothy, Chapter 5

Interesting advice here for presbyters or priests, as we would call them. In verses 17–25, the writer charts a very reasonable course for these servants of God. He seems to prefer that they take a moderate approach to spirituality. Don't get carried away. Don't get so focused on one thing that you lose sight of all the others. It's important in a position like this not to play favorites, although inevitably you will be more drawn to some people than others. It is sound advice for priests and ministers, but really it's good advice for all of us as we strive to live out our calling from God. This is a call that keeps coming, by the way. God has big plans for all of us. It just takes us awhile to figure them out. As we seek out our place in the Reign of God, we need to be mindful not to veer too much in any one direction.

Think About . . .

Why is it important not to get too carried away with your faith? What is the danger?

Today's Scripture Passage
1 Timothy, Chapter 6

Notice that there is more to verse 10, and that "more" makes a huge difference. The verse begins with the phrase "for the love of money," which puts a slant on this passage. Money in itself is neither good nor bad. It is a medium of exchange. Money can be used to accomplish great things. It can also be the motivation for crime and greed. We all need money to live in our society, and we can also help make a difference in the world by giving money to people and organizations that help others. Philanthropy is a wonderful force for good. It is when we love money, when it becomes our god, when we devote our lives to getting it, no matter what, that it becomes the source of evil. That is what we must avoid.

Think About . . .

Reflect on all the good that money can accomplish. How can you avoid falling in love with money?

Today's Scripture Passage
2 Timothy, Chapter 1

Verse 7 serves as a great reminder of what God's
Spirit can do within us. Timothy is told that we
are not given the Spirit to be timid or cowardly.
No, rather the Spirit fills us with power, love, and
self-control. This "trinity" of gifts is pretty amazing
when you think about it. We have power to really
make a positive difference in our world. If that
power comes from love, it will never be used to
hurt or oppress others. And if the power and love
that motivate us are teamed with self-control, we
will never go overboard in living out our Christian calling. Think about the evil that exists in our
world—war, terror, crime, abuse, exploitation. All
of these are distorted versions of power or love.
What is lacking is self-control, which holds the
forces of love and power in check. With God's
Spirit, we can counter the distortions of the world
and help love rule the day.

Think About . . .

Reflect on how the gifts of power, love, and
self-control operate in your life. Which could
you use more of?

Today's Scripture Passage

2 Timothy, Chapter 2

People get into arguments for all kinds of reasons. At times in Christian history, a single word or concept has created huge divisions in churches. In some ways, it all seems rather foolish, because in the end, we are all followers of the same Lord. Timothy, as a young church leader, is advised in verse 14 and in verses 23–24 to avoid the quarreling that can lead to more serious disputes that eventually split people apart. Some people are certainly more prone to quarreling than others, but the best course is to try to avoid disputes that are ultimately useless and divisive. Kindness is the best approach to dealing with quarrelsome people. And lots of patience. Gentleness can go a long way to diffusing a tense situation. A sense of humor also helps. Conflict is inevitable; arguing and fighting are not.

Think About . . .

Reflect on a recent quarrel or dispute you were involved in. Think about why it started and how it could have been avoided.

Today's Scripture Passage
2 Timothy, Chapters 3–4

It seems appropriate that on this last day of the year we end with Paul's final words to Timothy. There is a tone of both loneliness and resignation in Paul's writing as he wraps up his letter to Timothy. He has been through a lot and has been deserted by several companions. He knows the end is near. He also knows he has run the good race and has done his best. And really that is all God asks of us, isn't it? To do our best to be the best we can be. We are not Paul or Timothy, and we live in a very different time. But people haven't changed all that much. Friends will desert us and forget us. Life will be very hard at times, almost unbearable. Like Paul and like Timothy, we need to hang in there. A great victory awaits us at the finish line. God's grace provides the fuel to keep going. Ever onward!

Think About . . .

Look back over your year of walking with God's Word. How have you grown and changed through this experience?

Acknowledgments

The scriptural quotations labeled New Revised Standard Version or NRSV in the reflections for April 16, May 11, July 28, October 10, and October 27 are from the New Revised Standard Version of the Bible, Catholic Edition. Copyright © 1993 and 1989 by the Division of Christian Education of the National Council of the Churches of Christ in the United States of America. All rights reserved.

The scriptural quotations labeled Good News translation in the reflections for April 16 and October 28 are from the *Good News Bible* © 1994 published by the Bible Societies / HarperCollins Publishers, Ltd., *UK Good News Bible* © American Bible Society, 1966, 1971, 1976, 1992. Used with permission.

The scriptural quotations labeled New American Bible in the reflections for April 16 and October 13 are from the New American Bible with Revised New Testament and Revised Psalms. Copyright © 1991, 1986, and 1970 by the Confraternity of Christian Doctrine, Washington, D.C. Used by the permission of the copyright owner. All rights reserved. No part of the New American Bible may be reproduced in any form without permission in writing from the copyright owner.

The quotation in the reflection for May 18 is from *Catholic Household Blessings and Prayers*, by the Bishops' Committee on the Liturgy (Washington, DC: United States Conference of Catholic Bishops [USCCB], 1989), page 124. Copyright © 1989 by the USCCB. All rights reserved.

The quotations in the reflections for October 25 and November 25 are from the *Sacramentary*, English translation prepared by the International Commission on English in the Liturgy (New York: Catholic Book Publishing Company, 1985), page

During this book's preparation, all citations, facts, figures, names, addresses, telephone numbers, Internet URLs, and other pieces of information cited within were verified for accuracy. The authors and Saint Mary's Press staff have made every attempt to reference current and valid sources, but we cannot guarantee the content of any source, and we are not responsible for any changes that may have occurred since our verification. If you find an error in, or have a question or concern about, any of the information or sources listed within, please contact Saint Mary's Press.